MUSIC EXPLOSION

An Award-Winning Complete Early Childhood Curriculum
(includes a music CD* of all the songs in Music Explosion)

by
Stephanie K. Burton

Panda Bear Publications
P.O. Box 391
Manitou Springs, CO 80829
(ph) 719-685-3319; (fax) 719-685-4427
www.PandaBooks.com

*CD may be exchanged for audio cassette by mail. Send CD to :
Panda Bear Publications; PO Box 391; Manitou Springs, CO 80829

Acknowledgments

Thanks to:

Jane Neff for her expertise, encouragement, and guidance in writing this book;

Sam Hall of "Play It Again, Sam" for providing the musical notation;

Teachers Ellyn, Phyllis, Madeline, Penny, Sandy, Carol, Brenda, and Marilyn for reviewing my draft and encouraging me to finish;

The many children I have taught who have inspired me and made my job fun;

My parents, Lois and Norman Kay, who have always had confidence in me and helped me to follow my love of music;

Most of all, to my loving family, Andrew, Lindsey, and Joshua, for their patience and understanding while I worked on this book.

The purchase of this book entitles the owner to reproduce pages for use in an individual home, school, or child care center. Reproduction for use in an entire school system or chain of centers or for commercial use is prohibited. Beyond use as described above, no part of this publication may be transmitted or produced in any form by any means, electronic or mechanical, including photography, recording, or any information storage and retrieval system, without permission in writing from the publisher.

Copyright 1994. Perfection Learning Corporation

Copyright 2001. Panda Bear Publications;
PO Box 391; Manitou Springs, CO 80829
(719) 685-3319 ph   (719) 685-4427 fax
www.pandabooks.com

> Sing a song with children.
> Put music in their lives,
> And they'll bring joy to others
> As their voices harmonize.
> Stephanie Burton

About the Author

Stephanie K. Burton received her B.A. and M.A.T. from Colorado College. She teaches preschool in a public school, presents workshops on using music in the classroom, and performs with children.

Ms. Burton lives in Manitou Springs, Colorado, with her husband and two children. She enjoys hiking, riding bikes, singing, and playing guitar and piano with her family.

Contents

Introduction 6

A-B-C Song
A my name is ALICE by Jane Bayer 10

A-Hunting We Will Go
The Trek by Ann Jonas 16

Baby Bumblebee
Over in the Meadow illustrated by Ezra Jack Keats 20

The Bear Went Over the Mountain
Corduroy by Don Freeman 24

Bingo
Pet Show! by Ezra Jack Keats 28

De Colores
is it red? is it yellow? is it blue? by Tana Hoban 33

Down by the Bay
17 Kings and 42 Elephants by Margaret Mahy 42

The Eency Weency Spider
Anansi the Spider: a tale from the Ashanti adapted by Gerald McDermott 47

The Farmer in the Dell
The Farmer by Rosalinda Kightley 51

He's Got the Whole World
People by Peter Spier 56

Head, Shoulders, Knees, and Toes
Here Are My Hands by Bill Martin Jr. and John Archambault 60

Hickety Tickety Bumblebee
The Icky Bug Counting Book by Jerry Pallotta 65

Hickory Dickory Dock
Nicola Bayley's Book of Nursery Rhymes by Nicola Bayley . . . 69

If You're Happy and You Know It
the temper tantrum book by Edna Mitchell Preston 73

Jack and Jill
Tikki Tikki Tembo retold by Arlene Mosel 78

Johnny Hammers
Building a House by Byron Barton 82

Kumbaya
Ashanti to Zulu: African Traditions by Margaret Musgrove . . . 86

Little Bunny Foo Foo
Foolish Rabbit's Big Mistake by Rafe Martin 91

London Bridge
The Three Billy Goats Gruff retold by Paul Galdone 96

Mary's Wearing a Red Dress
Quick as a Cricket by Audrey Wood 100

Miss Polly Had a Dolly
The Berenstain Bears Go to the Doctor by Stan and Jan Berenstain 104

The More We Are Together
May I Bring a Friend? by Beatrice Schenk de Regniers 108

The Muffin Man
Martin's Hats by Joan W. Blos 113

Old MacDonald
Barn Dance! by Bill Martin Jr. and John Archambault 118

Pawpaw Patch
Growing Vegetable Soup by Lois Ehlert 123

Pop Goes the Weasel
The Elves and the Shoemaker retold by Freya Littledale 127

Ring Around the Rosy
Rosie's Walk by Pat Hutchins 131

Row, Row, Row Your Boat
Harbor by Donald Crews 135

Shalom Chavarim
It Could Always Be Worse retold by Margot Zemach 139

She'll Be Coming 'Round the Mountain
Things That Go by Anne Rockwell 144

There Was an Old Lady
I Know a Lady by Charlotte Zolotow 150

Twinkle, Twinkle Little Star
Grandfather Twilight by Barbara Berger 156

The Wheels on the Bus
Wheel Away! by Dayle Ann Dodds 160

Where Is Thumbkin?
Hand Rhymes by Marc Brown 165

Family Letter 169

Reproducible Take-Home Booklets 170

Glossary 204

Theme Index 206

Introduction

Children love music. They love singing songs, moving to music, and adding their own ideas and actions to make the music their own.

Music Explosion goes far beyond the scope of a songbook for teachers. It explains how teachers can take traditional children's songs and effectively use them to encourage and promote language development and creativity. The easy-to-use format encourages the teacher to use the music as a springboard into other curriculum areas such as science, math, art, reading/writing, social studies, and literature.

By using the timeless tunes that most of us grew up with, the teacher does not have to struggle with learning new songs. Many children may have already been exposed to this great wealth of music. Children's parents may also be familiar with these songs so that the music can easily be extended into the home.

Music can be a magical tool for teachers of young children. It can energize and motivate children or quiet them down and help them focus. Still, many teachers are reluctant to use music in their classrooms because they're not musicians, they can't sing, or they don't know the songs. For this reason, a cassette tape of the songs is provided. Just remember, however you choose to present the music, children will be accepting and noncritical. A teacher's enthusiasm alone can motivate an entire group of children to participate.

How to Use This Book

All of the activities in *Music Explosion* are developmentally appropriate for early childhood. Teachers are encouraged to choose those songs and activities that fit their teaching styles and the needs of their students.

Music Explosion contains 34 songs with curriculum extensions. Each song introduces a themed unit which includes the following components.

> The song in its traditional form. Each song has been musically notated in a range that is comfortable for the voices of young children. The music also includes easy chords for the guitar or autoharp.

> Music Expansion. This section provides suggestions for expanding on the music when singing with a group of children. These experiences are meant to encourage language development and creativity. Watch and listen to children as you sing with them. Be willing to try their ideas too, and you'll come up with a whole new repertoire!

A list of appropriate themes each song can introduce. You may already use some of these themes in your curriculum. The songs in *Music Explosion* can help you round out and extend that curriculum or can offer ideas for new themes.

A quality children's picture book to extend the song's main theme. This book may be read to the children and then used as a basis for activities in the Curriculum Integration section.

Curriculum Integration. This section extends the theme introduced by the song into curriculum areas. Each song can be used as a motivator for further exploration into science, math, art, reading/writing, and social studies. (Multicultural aspects have been incorporated into the activities when appropriate and relevant to the song and its theme.) You'll find the following curriculum areas in the Curriculum Integration:

- Science: Science experiences for young children need to include hands-on exploration and discovery. Children are invited to touch and explore during the science activities provided in *Music Explosion*. Young children enjoy a simplified form of the scientific process of prediction, observation, and hypothesis. With some activities it may help to keep a journal. Record children's predictions, observations, and hypotheses. Encourage children to dictate their entries to you, write their own entries, or use illustrations to convey their thoughts. However you decide to use journals, keep it simple and fun.

- Math: Just as in science, young children must experience concrete, hands-on math before they can successfully move on to the abstract paper-and-pencil types of math. Manipulatives such as counters, blocks, and unifix cubes are necessities in the math area. Math activities should be meaningful to young children and are most appropriate when used in play rather than practice and drill.

- Art: In order to promote creativity and self-esteem in young children, art activities should be process-oriented rather than product-oriented. Provide children with a variety of materials and media and encourage them to be creative. Some children will enjoy mixing, squishing, pouring, stamping, and pounding but may not be interested in producing what an adult might call a finished project. For this reason, traditional arts-and-crafts projects are best delayed until the child shows interest.

- Reading/Writing: Story time should be included as a definite component of the daily routine. Read to children often and encourage them to read or look at books on their own. Create an area in the room for reading that includes a child-size table and chairs, big pillows, good lighting, and plenty of theme-related books and child-created books.

  The writing activities should be modified to meet the needs and abilities of your children. Writing with three-, four-, and some five-year-olds consists of having them dictate to an adult or older child. The recorder should write exactly what the child says. Children who want to write by themselves should be encouraged to use invented spelling. Invite children to read their stories aloud to the class or small group. Or have children illustrate their stories and assemble the pages into books. Add the books to the classroom library.

- Social Studies: Many of the themes provide opportunities for children to learn more about themselves, their families, and the world around them. Suggestions are included for possible field trips, resource people, and classroom activities that will enhance themes and concepts in the songs.

A bibliography featuring related literature. The bibliography can be found at the end of each song's activities. These lists are just a sampling of what is available. Check your local library for both old favorites and new titles to enrich your curriculum.

A reproducible family letter. The letter explains to adults how to fold and use the minibooks with their children. It also offers suggestions for singing the song and reading the related book.

A reproducible minibook for each song. Each minibook in the back of this volume contains the song lyrics, a related activity, and the title of a picture book to be shared with the child. The minibooks are designed for children to take home to share with their families.

A glossary and theme index. The glossary defines some less familiar terms used in *Music Explosion*. The theme index makes it possible for teachers to start with a particular theme and then see which *Music Explosion* songs can be used to introduce or support the theme.

8

Enjoying Music with Young Children

Accept it as a given that children cannot sit still when they hear music, and your experience of using music with young children will be much happier and productive. As you sing with children, watch how they move, and listen to how they change the words. For example, if you're singing the song "Head, Shoulders, Knees, and Toes" and Jason insists on touching his back and waist, instead of viewing it as misbehavior, change the words so that everyone sings "Head, back and waist and toes." If you take cues from children, you will seldom have a discipline problem in group time. If children seem to be having too much trouble learning a song, find an easier one; if they're being fidgety or silly, put some movement into it.

When teaching a new song to children, the following steps will make it easier for both you and the children:

Step 1: Sing the song by yourself first. If some children already know the song, invite them to sing with you. If the song has motions, be sure to demonstrate them as you introduce the song.

Step 2: Echo Sing: Point to yourself as you sing a line or stanza; then point to children as they echo the same line. Do this until you have taught the entire song or until children seem comfortable singing it.

Step 3: Sing the song once again—all together this time.

Step 4: Expand on the traditional song by adding motions, changing words, varying the tempo or pitch, dramatizing, and/or using props.

Sometimes it will take only one day to reach step four. Often it may take two or three days depending on your group and the complexity of the song. Don't forget, children love repetition!

Most important of all, have fun! If you are enthusiastic and having fun with the music, it's guaranteed children will too.

Happy Singing,

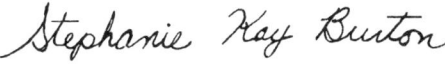

Stephanie Kay Burton

A-B-C Song

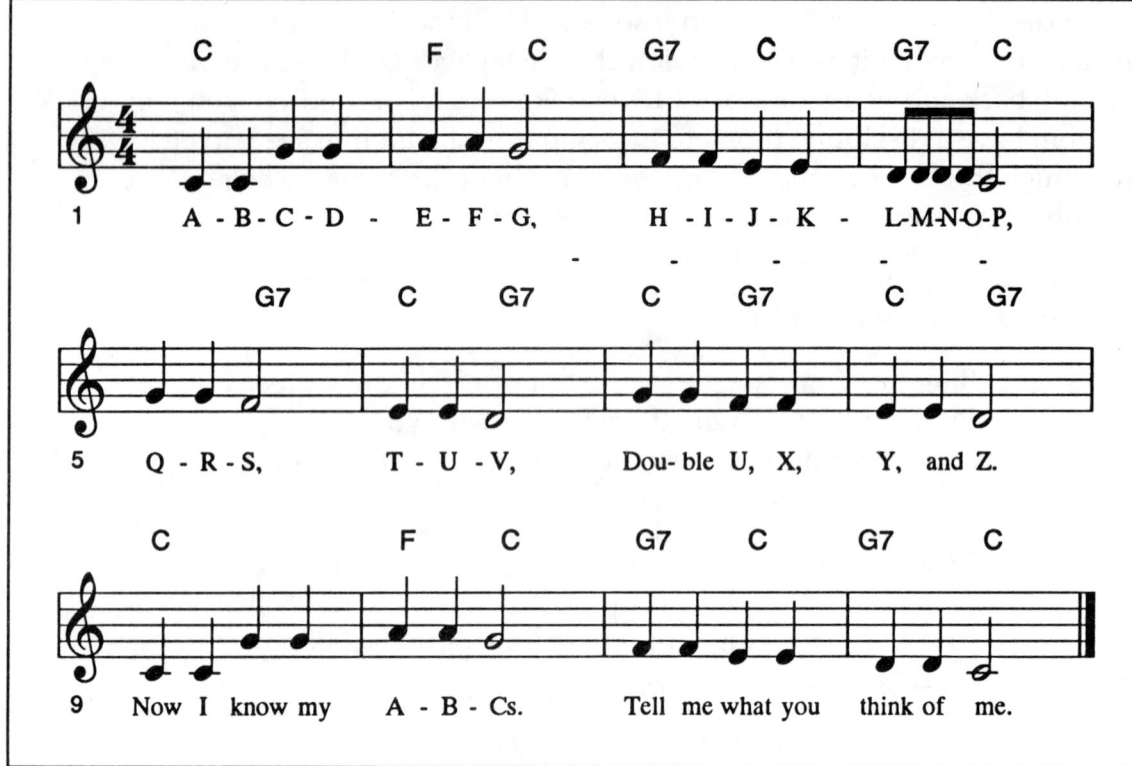

Music Expansion

Hand each child an alphabet letter card. Invite children to line up in alphabetical order as the song is sung.

Randomly distribute the alphabet letter cards. Ask each child to stand as his or her letter is named in the song.

Attach each alphabet letter card to a string so that the letters can be worn around children's necks. Give each child an instrument to play. As each letter is sung, the child with that letter plays the instrument.

As you sing the song, invite children to stand according to the first letter in their names.

Play a letter search game. As you sing the song, stop periodically. Have children identify the last letter sung and then locate that written letter somewhere in the room. Or suggest that they name someone or something which begins with the last letter sung.

Themes

Alphabet
Letters, Words, and Books

Featured Book

A my name is ALICE by Jane Bayer

Curriculum Integration

Choose activities from the following curriculum areas that fit your teaching style and the needs and interests of the children.

Science

Bury plastic or wooden letters in the sand table. Encourage children to identify the letters by touch before they uncover them. Suggest that they trace the letters in the sand or use the letters to make imprints.

Help children make bread dough using the recipe on the next page. Invite each child to take a small amount, knead it, and shape it into a letter. Then have children place their bread-dough letters on a cookie sheet and bake them according to recipe directions. When the letters are cool, invite children to eat them with margarine, cinnamon and sugar, or honey.

Bread Dough

Ingredients

1 package yeast
1 teaspoon salt
1 tablespoon sugar
1 1/2 cups warm water
4 cups flour

Utensils

measuring spoons
measuring cups
mixing bowl
mixing spoon
cookie sheet

Mix yeast, salt, and sugar in a mixing bowl. Stir in water. Mix well. Stir in flour. Knead on a floured surface. Form desired shape and place on a cookie sheet. Bake at 425°F for 12-15 minutes. Serve warm.

Math

Encourage children to measure, compare, and count while they are preparing the bread dough.

Provide two sets of alphabet letter cards. Invite children to match like letters. Some children may want to match lowercase letters with uppercase letters.

Make a graph of children's first initials. Write or have each child write his or her first name in a space above the appropriate letter. Then ask children to count the number of names in each column. Which column has the most names? Which column has the fewest names? Which columns have the same number of names? Display the graph in the math area. Encourage children to add to or revise the graph as the class changes. The graph might look like the one on the next page.

	Chelsea			
	Charles			
Anton	Christy		Mary	
Adam	Carmen		Marc	
Angie	Carlos		Mitch	Robert
Alison	Carol	Eddie	Marian	Rachel
A	C	E	M	R

Reading/Writing

Read *A my name is ALICE*. Help children notice that the words in the book are made from a combination of alphabet letters. Invite them to point out any letters or words that are familiar to them.

Point out the author's name, Jane Bayer, on the cover of the book *A my name is ALICE*. Explain that an *author* is a person who uses letters and words to write a book or story. Then invite children to become authors and create their own group story. Have children take turns creating sentences or phrases. Write their responses on a large sheet of chart paper. Encourage children to continue until they decide the story is finished. (Read the story at intervals to remind children what has already been dictated.) Read the final story to them. Encourage children to point out letters and words they recognize.

Invite children to write and illustrate their own stories using invented spelling. Suggest that they make a cover and staple it and the story pages together for a book. Encourage volunteers to read their stories to the class or group. Make a library of the books children create.

Art

Invite children to select a letter of the alphabet and turn it into a picture. For example, some children might make a *V* into an ice cream cone or an *O* into a flower center.

Invite children to make a letter collage. Have them trace letters onto sheets of construction paper and cut them out. Then encourage them to use scraps of fabric, seeds, cotton balls, or other collage materials to decorate their letters. Suggest that children glue their letters to a large sheet of mural paper. When the collage is finished, display it on a bulletin board or wall.

Point out the illustrator's name, Steven Kellogg, on the cover of *A my name is ALICE*. Explain that an *illustrator* is a person who draws pictures for a book or story. Invite children to talk about what they like or don't like about the illustrations in this book. Then suggest that children become illustrators. Invite them to create illustrations for the group story they write as a reading/writing activity. Provide paper and encourage children to choose one or more media to create their illustrations. Display the story and illustrations in a prominent place. Encourage children to discuss how the illustrations help make the reader understand the words and letters in a story or book.

Social Studies

Invite children to go on a walk around the school or neighborhood. Have children identify objects that begin with each letter of the alphabet. Or provide pairs of children with alphabet letter cards. Encourage each pair to point out objects that begin with the letter.

Explain that reading and writing are necessary for most jobs. Have children ask parents or other adults how letters are important to them and the jobs they do. Then encourage children to share their findings with the class or group. Children may also want to invite parents or other adults to visit with the class about how they use letters, reading, and writing.

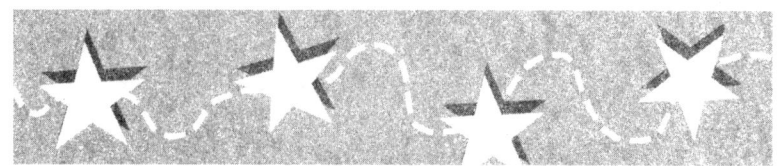

Related Literature

A my name is ALICE by Jane Bayer. This alphabet book features animals with unique qualities. Holt, 1991.

Animal Alphabet by Bert Kitchen. A wordless picture book shows majestic paintings of animals from *armadillo* to *zebra*. Dial, 1988.

Anno's Alphabet Book by Mitsumasa Anno. This wordless picture book is filled with playful, bold images of each letter of the alphabet and illustrations that abound with surprises and visual puns. HarperCollins, 1988.

jambo means hello: Swahili Alphabet Book by Muriel Feelings. From A to Z, illustrated Swahili words re-create the traditions of East Africa. Dial, 1985.

A Northern Alphabet by Ted Harrison. The northern regions of the world are explored in this brightly illustrated alphabet book. Tundra, 1989.

The Underwater Alphabet Book by Jerry Pallotta. Go underwater to explore the coral reef, from Angelfish to Zebra Pipefish, in this alphabet book in which amazing tropical creatures lead the reader through an important ecological system. Charlesbridge, 1991.

A-Hunting We Will Go

1 A-hunt-ing we will go. A-hunt-ing we will go. We'll
6 catch a fox and put him in a box, and then we'll let him go.

Additional verses

. . . catch a pig and put him in a wig . . .

. . . catch a turtle and put her in a girdle . . .

Music Expansion

Invite two children to form a bridge by facing each other and holding each other's hands in the air—similar to the action in "London Bridge." Have the other children stand in a line and walk under the bridge. On the words *catch a fox*, the two children drop their hands to capture the child walking under. As children sing *and then we'll let him go*, children raise their hands.

Suggest that children make up new rhymes for the song. Talk about rhyming words such as *fox* and *box*, *pig* and *wig*, and *turtle* and *girdle*. Some examples might include *dog* and *log*, *mouse* and *house*, or *whale* and *jail*.

Have children act out the song with one child as the "hunter" and the other children as the animal to be caught. Encourage the "animals" to move the way they think the real animal would.

Themes
Animals
Endangered Species
Habitats
Rhyming Words

Featured Book
The Trek by Ann Jonas

Curriculum Integration
Choose activities from the following curriculum areas that fit your teaching style and the needs and interests of the children.

Science
Explain that *endangered animals* are animals that may become extinct like the dinosaurs. Ask children to discuss why they think some animals are endangered. Talk about how scientists often capture endangered animals in order to study them and to help save the species. Invite children to think of ways to help endangered animals.

Provide children with pictures of animals. Have children discuss where the animals might be found. Some might be found on farms, some in jungles, or some in deserts.

Read *The Trek*. Invite children to look closely at the illustrations and identify any animals they see. Point out that the animals are often hard to see because of *camouflage*. Explain that camouflage is the coloring and markings of animals that make them look like their surroundings. Camouflage helps hide animals from their enemies. Have children look at the illustrations again, find an animal, and tell what the animal resembles.

Math
Set out toy animals and containers. Invite children to count how many animals fit in each size container. Suggest that children sort animals by color, size, type, or other methods of classification.

Bring in different types and sizes of boxes such as an appliance box, a grocery store box, a shoe box, and a jewelry box. Ask children to name animals they think would fit in each of the boxes. Encourage children to talk about why they matched a certain animal to a particular box.

Art

Offer children tape, glue, scissors, and boxes of various sizes and shapes. Then invite them to work in groups to create boxes to hold animals. Remind children to think about the animals they are making the box for. Do the animals have special features that need a special shape of box?

Invite children to look at Ms. Jonas' illustrations in *The Trek* and notice how she blended the animals into the surroundings. Provide children with sheets of drawing paper. Encourage them to draw animals and then blend them into the surroundings. Display the pictures in the science area on a Camouflage bulletin board.

Reading/Writing

Invite children to use *The Trek* to tell their own stories. Have each child show a picture in the book and make up a story to go with it. Provide a tape recorder for those children who wish to record their original stories.

Develop a rhyme bank for different animals. Write an animal's name at the top of a sheet of chart paper. Then invite children to suggest words that rhyme with the animal's name. Do this for several animals and hang the charts in the language arts area. Have children create new verses for the song using rhymes from the charts. Suggest they draw pictures showing the new verses and dictate or write the verses on the pictures. Bind the pictures together to form an *A-Hunting I Will Go* book.

Social Studies

Invite children to go on a trek. Explain that a *trek* is a journey or a trip. Arrange a visit to a zoo or nature center. Encourage children to "hunt" for animals that appear in the book. If possible, take along a camera and "catch" some of the animals on film.

Related Literature

Hide-and-Seek on the Farm by Laura Damon. As the barnyard animals play hide-and-seek, it's fun to join in by helping find them. Troll, 1987.

Lily Takes a Walk by Satoshi Kitamura. A girl and her dog see different things on their evening walk. Dutton, 1987.

1 Hunter by Pat Hutchins. A hilarious hunter walks through the jungle, making a true adventure out of hunting. Morrow, 1982.

The Trek by Ann Jonas. A little girl sees some amazing things during an ordinary walk to school. Greenwillow, 1985.

Will We Miss Them? Endangered Species by Alexandra Wright. This intriguing collection contains fascinating facts about the lives and challenges of endangered species. Charlesbridge, 1991.

With Love from Gran by Dick Gackenbach. A little boy's grandmother decides to see the world and sends him a present from each place she visits. Clarion, 1989.

Baby Bumblebee

Additional verses

I'm bringing home a baby dinosaur.
Won't my mommy just go through the floor,
'Cause I'm bringing home a baby dinosaur.
Stomp, stomp, stomp, stomp.
OUCH! He crushed me!

I'm bringing home a baby rattlesnake.
Won't my mommy just think that is great,
'Cause I'm bringing home a baby rattlesnake.
S-s-s-s-s-s-s-s-s
GULP! He swallowed me!

Music Expansion

Invite children to clap with the rhythm of the song.

Provide rhythm instruments. Encourage children to use the instruments to keep time with the music. Suggest that they experiment with the instruments to imitate baby animal sounds. For example, a stick and sandpaper block could be used for the bee sound and a drum could be used for the dinosaur sound.

Invite children to act out the verses. Encourage them to move like the animals in the verses. Have children imagine what it would be like to bring home a bumblebee, dinosaur, rattlesnake, or other animal. Suggest that children make up new verses and act those out also.

Themes

Animals
Habitats

Featured Book

Over in the Meadow illustrated by Ezra Jack Keats

Curriculum Integration

Choose activities from the following curriculum areas that fit your teaching style and the needs and interests of the children.

Science

Explain that a *meadow* is an area of land that is grassy. Point out that the land is often low and wet. Ask children what animals they think might live in a meadow. Then read *Over in the Meadow*. Invite children to discuss what animals are shown in the book.

Obtain a tadpole from a pond or pet store. Set aside an area in the science center for a small, shallow aquarium. Make paper, markers, crayons, and pencils available for children to draw and/or write about their observations as the tadpole changes. Date the papers and bind them together when the project is completed. When the tadpole has grown into a frog, take it to a nearby pond or stream and release it.

Math

Provide flannel board pictures of animals and their young. Encourage children to match the young with the adults and count all the animals. Some children might count by twos. Suggest children take one or more animals away and count how many are left.

Invite children to classify plastic animals by color, size, and where they might be found such as a farm, the woods, or a zoo. Have children place the animals in a line and tell which is first, which is last, and which is in the middle.

Art

Display *Over in the Meadow* and point out that it was illustrated by Ezra Jack Keats. Encourage children to talk about the illustrations. Then invite children to use watercolors or thinned tempera paints, brushes, and sponges to create pictures of areas where animals might live. When the pictures are dry, suggest children cut out magazine pictures of animals that would live in the areas they painted. Have them glue the animals to their pictures. Display the pictures on a wall or bulletin board.

Ask children what baby animal they would like to bring home. Invite them to use a variety of art media to create pictures showing themselves and the animals. Then encourage each child to write or dictate something about the animal and how an adult might react to having the animal at home.

Reading/Writing

Read *Over in the Meadow*. Then suggest that children make up verses for "Baby Bumblebee" using animals from the book.

Invite children to study one of the animals they have sung about in the song or read about in the book. Have children brainstorm everything they know about that animal. Write the responses on chart paper. Encourage children to look for books about the animal in the library. If possible, invite a conservation officer or another authority on animals to visit and talk about the animal. As children learn more about the animal, record the additional information on the chart. At the end of the unit, invite children to write a class story about the animal.

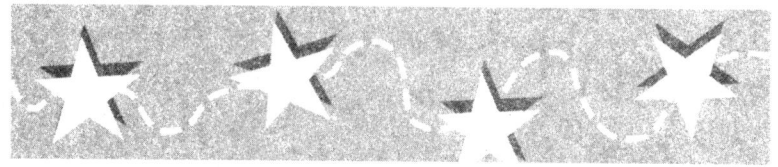

Social Studies

Visit a science center or wildlife preserve, or invite someone in to talk about the wildlife in the area. Suggest that the speaker bring pictures of the animals and their young. Encourage children to watch for some of the animals when they are traveling to and from school or playing outside.

Related Literature

Annie and the Wild Animals by Jan Brett. When Annie's cat disappears, she attempts friendship with a variety of woodland animals. Houghton Mifflin, 1985.

Baby Animals. This book gives factual information about baby animals. Price, Stern, and Sloan, 1984.

It Does Not Say Meow and Other Animal Riddle Rhymes by Beatrice Schenk de Regniers. This book focuses on nine favorite and familiar animals ranging from an ant to an elephant. Houghton Mifflin, 1983.

Over in the Meadow illustrated by Ezra Jack Keats. This classic Appalachian counting rhyme gradually reveals layers and layers of sand and grass, where mothers and babies live in their unique meadow habitats. Scholastic, 1986.

Who Lives Here? by Dot and Sy Barlowe. Seven environments from pond to prairie—and more than 100 animals that inhabit them—are described in clear text and large, realistic pictures. Random, 1980.

The Bear Went Over the Mountain

Music Expansion

Invite children to dramatize the song. Have children take turns climbing an imaginary mountain or an indoor or outdoor climber. When each child reaches the top, ask what's on the other side of the mountain. Encourage the group to sing about what the child "sees."

Sing about other animals going over the mountain instead of the bear. For example, the bird flew over the mountain, the snake slithered over the mountain, or the turtle crawled over the mountain. Invite children to move like the different animals as they sing the verses.

Themes

Bears
Habitats
Hibernation

Featured Book

Corduroy by Don Freeman

Curriculum Integration

Choose activities from the following curriculum areas that fit your teaching style and the needs and interests of the children.

Science

Invite children to learn about bears. Set up a discovery table in the science area. Provide books, magazines, and other materials about bears. Encourage children to bring in related items and books to add to the discovery table. Suggest that children spend time studying the items.

Read *Corduroy*. Remind children that Corduroy wants a home. Ask children to describe Corduroy's new home. Then show children pictures showing real bears' homes from books or magazines such as *World* or *Ranger Rick*. Have children talk about the similarities and differences between Corduroy's home and a real bear's home.

Point out that bears spend the winters hibernating in caves. Explain that *to hibernate* means to sleep soundly during winter. Animals that hibernate only wake up occasionally to look for food. Ask children if they know of any other animals that hibernate besides bears. Make a list of the animals to display in the science area.

Math

Place bear counters and bowls in the math area and invite children to turn the bowls upside down to make mountains. Suggest they match bears according to size or to the color of the "mountains." Numerals can be written on the bowls indicating how many bears can climb that mountain. Encourage children to tell stories as they sort and match.

Provide a balance with the bear counters. Encourage children to experiment with the concepts of *heavier* or *lighter* and *more* or *less*.

Art

Ask children what they think the bear saw on the other side of the mountain. Then ask children to pretend they're taking a walk and they turn a corner. Invite them to draw a picture of what they might see around the corner. Suggest children write or dictate something about their pictures. Display the pictures on a bulletin board titled "Children Went 'Round the Corner."

Remind children that Corduroy goes to live with Lisa in her home. Invite children to cut out pictures of people's and animals' homes. Have each child make a home collage by gluing pictures to sheets of construction paper.

Reading/Writing

Invite children to write or dictate individual or class stories about the bear. Some story starters might include

The bear went over the ocean . . .

The bear went up to the moon . . .

The bear went to visit the president . . .

Read other stories about bears. Ask children what they would do if they met a real bear. Invite them to brainstorm a list of safety rules for anyone who might encounter a bear or other wild animal.

Social Studies

Arrange a field trip to the zoo. Encourage children to talk about their observations of the bears. Write down their responses. When the class returns, transfer children's comments to chart paper and read them to children. Encourage children to add to or revise the comments.

Related Literature

Bears. This book gives factual information about bears. Price, Stern, and Sloan, 1984.

Blueberries for Sal by Robert McCloskey. What happens when a little girl and a bear cub stray from their mothers' sides? Viking, 1948.

Corduroy by Don Freeman. A toy bear who wants to find a home and someone who loves him eventually does. Penguin, 1976.

The Happy Day by Ruth Krauss. The forest animals celebrate spring by coming out of hibernation. HarperCollins, 1949.

Where Are My Bears? by Ron Hirschi. Young readers explore mountains and forests, and they are introduced to ecology and what can be done to save endangered species. Bantam, 1992.

Bingo

Additional verses

There was a farmer had a dog,
And Bingo was his name-o.
(clap)-I-N-G-O,
(clap)-I-N-G-O,
(clap)-I-N-G-O,
And Bingo was his name-o.

. . . (clap, clap)-N-G-O . . .

. . . (clap, clap, clap)-G-O . . .

. . . (clap, clap, clap, clap)-O . . .

. . . (clap, clap, clap, clap, clap) . . .

Music Expansion

Write the letters *B-I-N-G-O* on the chalkboard. Invite children to take turns erasing each letter as it is eliminated in the song.

Ask children what other kind of animal Bingo could be. Then ask them how the song could be changed to use other animals. Would a farmer have a lion? How would they change the words?

Invite children to sing about pets. For example,

> I know Terry has a cat,
> And Cuddles is its name-o.

(Squeeze in the extra letters to make the song work.)

Have children play instruments to replace the letters of the song. Or children could use certain instruments to represent each letter. For example, rhythm sticks could be played for the letter *B*.

Themes

Animals
Pets/Pet Care

Featured Book

Pet Show! by Ezra Jack Keats

Curriculum Integration

Choose activities from the following curriculum areas that fit your teaching style and the needs and interests of the children.

Science

Adopt a classroom pet and name it Bingo. Talk with children about the needs of the pet. Help them set up a care schedule.

Invite children to look at pictures of each other's pets. Encourage children to talk about how the pets are similar and different.

Math

After children have sung the song several times, invite them to play a clapping game. Have them listen while you clap a pattern such as clap, pause, clap. Then ask them to repeat the pattern exactly as you did it. Continue creating patterns for children to repeat.

Invite children to make a graph showing what pets they have. The graph might look like the one below.

🐕	Sue	Ken	Maria	
🐈	Maria	Jim	Bill	Tracy
🐟	Joe	Aaron		
🐦	Lisa	Tracy		

Then ask questions about the graph such as "What kind of pet do most children have?"

Invite children to play a Bingo game with colors, shapes, letters, numbers, or animals.

Read *Pet Show!* Then invite children to bring in stuffed animals or toys for a "pet show." Have children compare the toys. Remind children that the pets in the book received awards for such qualities as being the noisiest parrot, the friendliest fishes, and the brightest goldfish. Ask children to identify qualities that the stuffed toys have such as the longest tail.

Art

Provide collage materials, markers, crayons, paper bags, and old socks. Then invite children to make sack or sock puppets of pets.

Read *Pet Show!* Point out that each pet receives an award. Invite children to create awards for pets they own or would like to own. Have children share their awards with the class and explain what the awards are for and why their pets would get them.

Reading/Writing

After reading *Pet Show!* aloud to children, have them design an Our Pets bulletin board. Suggest that children bring in photos of their pets. Mount each photo on construction paper and have each child write or dictate something about the pet.

If you have a classroom pet, encourage children to keep a daily or weekly journal of the pet's activities. Suggest children write, dictate, or draw their observations.

Write each of the letters *B, I, N, G,* and *O* on separate sheets of chart paper. Invite children to think of words that begin with each letter sound. Write the words under the appropriate letters. Add to the charts as children think of other words.

Social Studies

Talk about pet care. Visit an animal shelter in your community or have a representative come in and talk to your class. Encourage children to ask questions about pet care.

Arrange a field trip to a pet store. Help children notice all the pet-care products that are available.

Help children set up a pet store in the dramatic play area. Provide a cash register; play money; pet supplies such as old collars, leashes, brushes, and toys; and stuffed animals. Encourage children to make signs for the store. Suggest that children take turns being salespeople and customers.

Related Literature

Annie's Pet by Barbara Brenner. A young girl takes her five birthday dollars to spend on a pet. She ends up with a lot more—and less—than she bargained for. Bantam, 1989.

Can I Keep Him? by Steven Kellogg. A little boy tries to convince his mother to let him have a pet. Dial, 1978.

Clifford, the Big Red Dog by Norman Bridwell. A little girl and a giant dog named Clifford have some exciting adventures. Scholastic, 1985.

Duncan and Dolores by Barbara Samuels. Dolores learns to curb some of her more smothering tendencies and wins the affection of her new pet cat, Duncan. Aladdin, 1989.

Harry, the Dirty Dog by Gene Zion. Harry hates baths so much that one day he buries the scrubbing brush in the backyard and runs away from home. HarperCollins, 1976.

Pet Show! by Ezra Jack Keats. How can Archie enter a pet show when his pet runs away? Macmillan, 1972.

De Colores

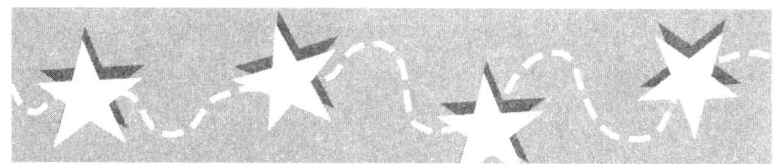

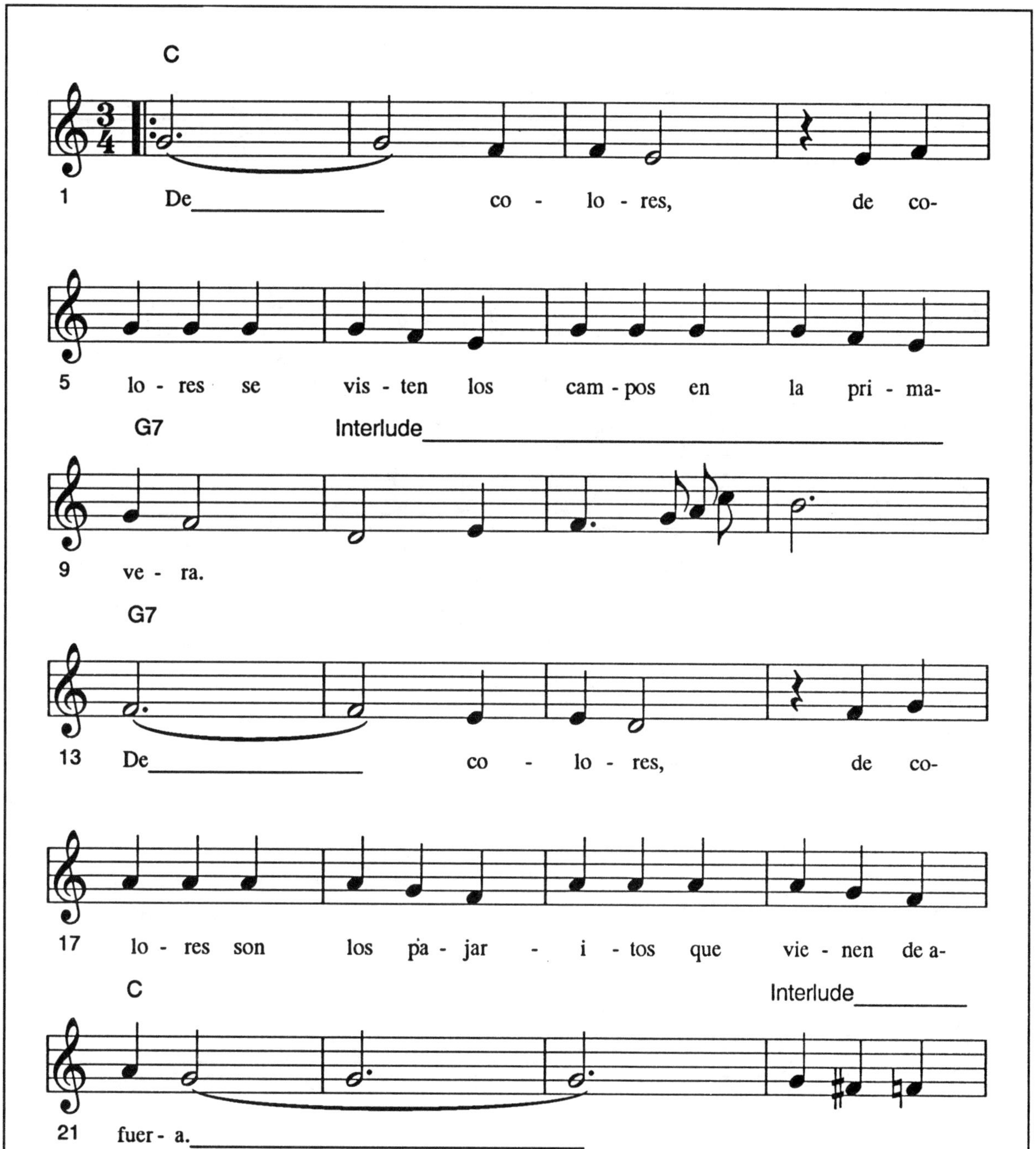
C
1 De co - lo - res, de co-
5 lo - res se vis - ten los cam - pos en la pri - ma-
G7
Interlude
9 ve - ra.
G7
13 De co - lo - res, de co-
17 lo - res son los pa - jar - i - tos que vie - nen de a-
C
Interlude
21 fuer - a.

De Colores (continued)

De Colores (continued)

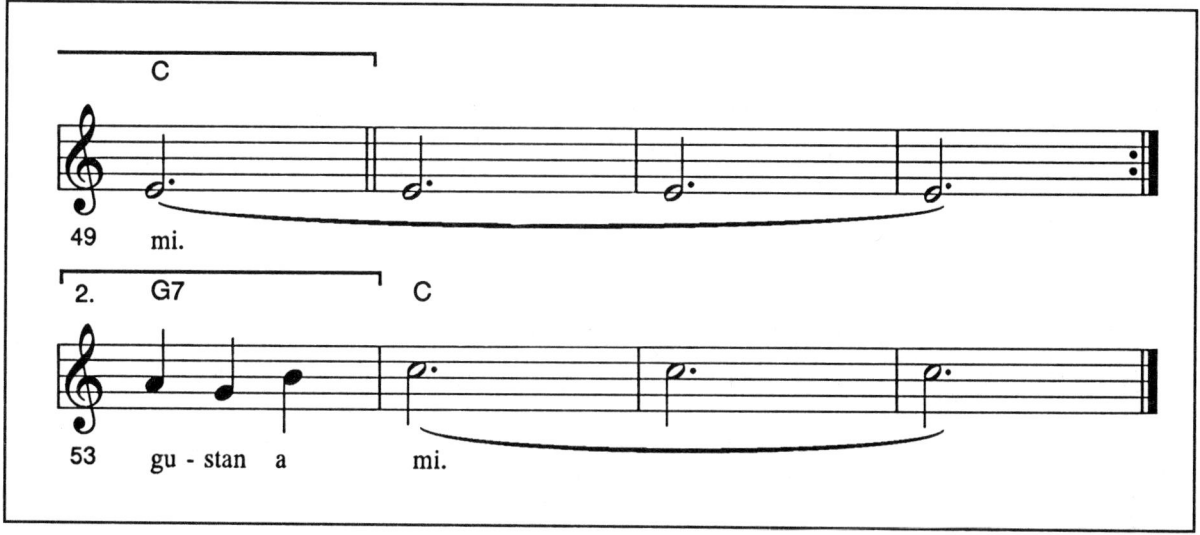

Additional verse

Canta el gallo,
Canta el gallo con el quiri, quiri, quiri, quiri, quiri;
La gallina.
La gallina con la cara, cara, cara, cara, cara;
Los polluelos,
Los polluelos con el pio, pio, pio, pio, pio;
Y por eso los grandes amores
De muchos colores me gustan a mi.
Y por eso los grandes amores
De muchos colores me gustan a mi.

Music Expansion

Explain that this song is sung in Spanish. The first verse is about colors—the colors of the fields in springtime, the birds that fly around outside, and a rainbow that shines. The second verse is about a rooster (el gallo), a hen (la gallina), chicks (los polluelos), and the sounds each animal makes. Help children notice that the words for the sounds the animals make are different in Spanish than in English.

Suggest that children listen to "De Colores" and think about how the song makes them feel. Then provide children with streamers of material

or crepe paper and invite them to perform a color dance. Encourage them to gently wave their streamers and move to the music.

Themes

Colors
Counting/Numbers
Cultures

Featured Book

is it red? is it yellow? is it blue? by Tana Hoban

Curriculum Integration

Choose activities from the following curriculum areas that fit your teaching style and the needs and interests of the children.

Math

Make muffin crayons with the class. Have children place two cupcake papers in each cup of a muffin tin. (Several tins may be needed depending on the number of crayons you have.) Ask children to remove wrappers from broken crayons and then sort them by color into the various cups. Don't overfill the cups. Suggest they place mixed crayons in one or two cups. Follow the directions given in science and then use the muffin crayons in Art.

Invite children to count to ten in Spanish. Then encourage children to count objects in the room in both English and Spanish. They might count children, days on the calendar, chairs, or windows.

one	uno
two	dos
three	tres
four	cuatro
five	cinco

six	seis
seven	siete
eight	ocho
nine	nueve
ten	diez

Make a graph of children's favorite colors. Then help children draw conclusions by asking questions and encouraging them to explain their answers. Some questions might include

Which color is the most popular?

Which color is least popular?

Were any colors not listed?

Science

Invite children to make tortillas using the following recipe.

Tortillas

Ingredients

2 cups flour
1 teaspoon salt
1 cup warm water

Utensils

measuring cups
measuring spoons
bowl
rolling pin

Mix flour and salt in a bowl. Add water and stir until dough holds its shape. Add extra flour or water if needed. Divide dough into twelve small pieces. Roll the dough into balls and then flatten the balls with the palms of the hand or a rolling pin. Heat the tortillas in a warm oven or on a griddle until lightly browned on both sides.

Help children measure the ingredients. Encourage them to talk about changes they observe when the ingredients are combined and as the tortillas cook. Serve the tortillas with butter or margarine, honey, or jam. Or make quesadillas. Have children sprinkle the tortillas with shredded cheese and put them on a cookie sheet. Place the cookie sheet in a 350°F oven or under a broiler until the cheese is melted.

Invite children to make muffin crayons. Have children place old crayon pieces in muffin cups. (See Math.) Then ask children what they think will happen when the crayons are placed in an oven. Record their predictions on chart paper. Then place the muffin tins in a 350°F oven for ten minutes or until the crayons have melted together and taken the shape of the muffin cup. Carefully remove the muffin tins from the oven and let them cool. Have children observe the changes and talk about their predictions.

Art

After the muffin crayons have cooled, have children carefully remove the cupcake papers. Place a large sheet of butcher paper or mural paper on the floor. Invite children to draw with the muffin crayons as they listen to various types of music. Encourage children to talk about how the different types of music make them feel as they draw.

Show children the book *is it red? is it yellow? is it blue?* Explain that these colors are called *primary* colors and that all other colors are made from combinations of these three colors and black and white. Invite children to experiment making colors. Provide paper, tempera paints or watercolors in primary colors, and brushes. Have children blend colors on paper and talk about what other colors they make.

Explain that often flowers are sold in a Mexican marketplace or *mercado*. Then invite children to make flowers to decorate the room. For each flower, cut four to six sheets of tissue paper into 6" x 12" rectangles. Have children choose the colors they want, lay the papers on top of each other, and fold them accordion-style starting at the narrow end. Then help the children pinch the papers in the middle and secure with flower wire (available from a craft shop) or with chenille stems. Have each child pull one sheet at a time toward the center to form the flower petals. Hang the flowers around the room.

Tissue Paper Flower

Step 1

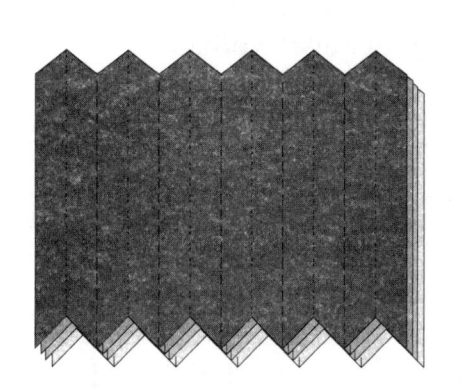

Step 2

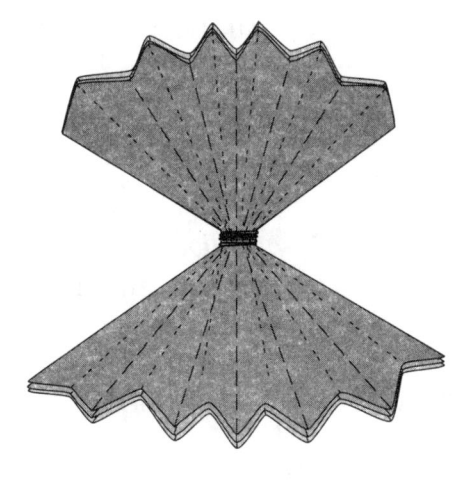

Step 3

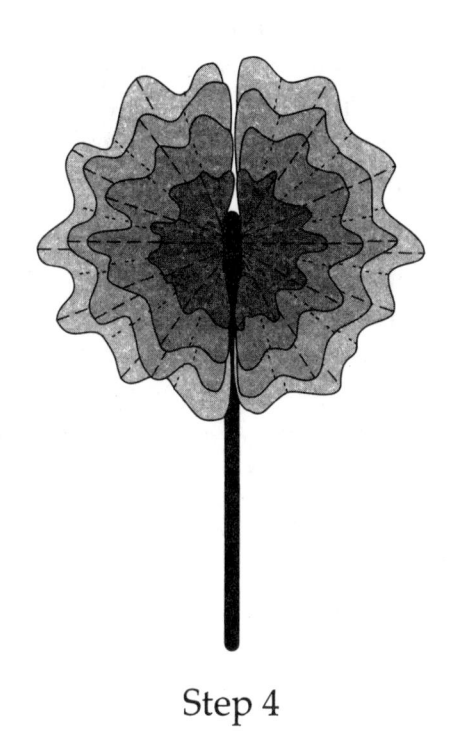

Step 4

39

Reading/Writing

Read *is it red? is it yellow? is it blue?* to children. Then choose the most popular color from the color graph. (See Math.) Ask children to brainstorm a list of everything they can think of that is that color. Record their responses on chart paper. Suggest children color pictures of some of the things on the chart. Display the chart and the pictures on a wall or bulletin board.

Invite children to write a book about colors. On sheets of drawing paper, write color words in English and Spanish. Say the Spanish word and invite children to say it also. Then have each child choose a color and dictate or write something about the color. Have children illustrate the pages with watercolor paintings, or crayon or chalk drawings. Suggest they write the English and Spanish words for the colors. Bind the pages together to make a color book for the class library.

red	rojo
blue	azul
green	verde
yellow	amarillo
orange	naranja

brown	moreno
black	negro
purple	purpurado
pink	rosado
white	blanco

Social Studies

Remind children that the objects in the book *is it red? is it yellow? is it blue?* were found in the community. Invite children to go for a walk in the neighborhood. Have them look for objects which are red, yellow, or blue. Or play a color game. Call out a color and encourage children to identify as many objects as they can before you call another color.

Show children where Mexico is located on a large map. Then point out where you live. Have children compare the size and shape of Mexico to their state or province.

Explain that Cinco de Mayo (May 5) is one of Mexico's most important holidays. It celebrates the winning of the battle against the French on May 5, 1862, which led to Mexican independence. The holiday is similar to the Fourth of July in the United States. It is celebrated in Mexico and by Mexican Americans with a fiesta of music, dance, and feasts.

Invite students and their families to a Mexican fiesta with Mexican food, music, and a piñata to break. Suggest that families provide food, and you can provide the music and a place for the fun. Purchase a piñata at a party goods store or have children make one out of papier mâché.

Related Literature

The Color Wizard by Barbara Brenner. The story takes the reader through a colorless kingdom gradually transformed to a rainbow-colored spectrum by a wizard named Gray. Bantam, 1989.

Colors by John J. Reiss. Eight colors are represented in illustrations of animals, foods, insects, and flowers. Macmillan, 1982.

Count Your Way Through Mexico by Jim Haskins. This book presents the numbers 1 to 10 in Spanish as well as facts about the history, culture, and climate of Mexico. Carolrhoda, 1989.

Hello, Amigos! by Tricia Brown. The everyday life of a Mexican-American boy living in the Mission District of San Francisco is captured through photos as he anticipates his upcoming birthday and celebrates it according to his culture's customs. Holt, 1986.

is it red? is it yellow? is it blue? by Tana Hoban. This concept book explores colors, sizes, and shapes. Morrow, 1978.

Down by the Bay

Down by the bay, where the wa-ter-mel-ons grow, back to my home, I dare not go, for if I do, my moth-er will say, "Did you ev-er see a goose kiss-ing a moose down by the bay?"

Additional verses

... whale with a polka-dot tail ...

... fly wearing a tie ...

... bear combing his hair ...

... llamas eating their pajamas ...

Music Expansion

Encourage children to make up motions to go with the last line of the song.

Provide flannel board pictures of various animals and things that rhyme with each animal's name. Encourage children to match the pictures as they sing verses to the song.

Themes

Animals
Bodies of Water
Counting/Numbers
Growing Things
Rhyming Words

Featured Book

17 Kings and 42 Elephants by Margaret Mahy

Curriculum Integration

Choose activities from the following curriculum areas that fit your teaching style and the needs and interests of the children.

Science

Explain that a *bay* is a body of water that is partially surrounded by land but opens to the ocean on one side. Display a map of North America and point out several bays such as Chesapeake Bay on the Massachusetts coast and Hudson Bay in Canada. Ask children what they think might be found in and around a bay. What types of animals, plants, and transportation might be seen?

Invite children to plant watermelon seeds using a variety of soil types such as sand, potting soil, or dirt from the playground. Encourage children to tend and observe the plants. Provide journals so they can record their observations with drawings and dictated or written sentences. After several weeks, ask children what conclusions they might make about the plants and the soils they were grown in.

Fill the water table or a large tub with water. Provide children with measuring cups, different sizes of containers, and sink-and-float items. Encourage children to talk about what they observe about water.

Math

Serve watermelon at snack time and invite children to count how many watermelon seeds each piece has. Make a graph of the numbers and then ask children questions about the results. Who had the most seeds? Who had the fewest seeds? Did any children have the same number of seeds?

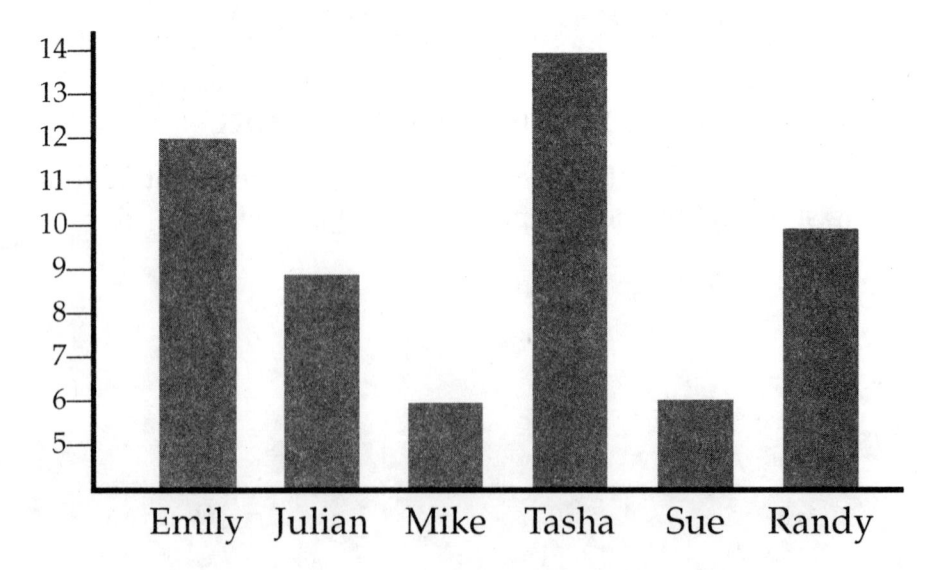

Read *17 Kings and 42 Elephants*. Point out the first two pages of the story. Ask children to estimate how many elephants and how many kings are on the two pages. Then help children count the elephants and kings. Were their estimates larger, smaller, or about the same? Continue the activity with other pages of the book.

Art

Show the illustrations in *17 Kings and 42 Elephants*. Encourage children to talk about the illustrations and how they compare with other books' illustrations. (Have other books available for children to look at.)

Write each verse for "Down by the Bay" at the bottom of a large sheet of drawing paper. Invite children to illustrate the verses using markers, crayons, paints, pencils, torn paper, and other art media. Bind the pages together to make a big book.

Reading/Writing

Invite children to create new verses for the song. Ask children to think of animals and then think of rhymes for each animal mentioned. Create a rhyme bank by writing the suggested animals and rhymes on chart paper. Then encourage children to create new verses for the song using words from the rhyme bank.

Read *17 Kings and 42 Elephants*. Help children notice the rhymes at the ends of the lines. Then have them point out made-up words that the author uses to describe the animals in the book. For example, the author uses the word *umbrellaphants* to describe the elephants' ears. Ask children what they think the made-up words mean. Then have them make up words of their own to describe things.

Social Studies

Remind children that a bay is mentioned in the song and a river is mentioned in *17 Kings and 42 Elephants*. Ask children to brainstorm a list of bodies of water. Help them find pictures of these in magazines and books or on maps. Have children compare the sizes and shapes of different bodies of water. If possible, take children on a field trip to a nearby body of water. Encourage them to talk about the characteristics. Is it completely surrounded by land? What is the land near the water like? Are there any animals nearby?

Related Literature

Down by the Bay by Raffi. Down by the bay, two young friends make up fantastic rhymes, each trying to top the other. Crown, 1987.

Jamberry by Bruce Degen. A bear that speaks in nonsense verse guides a young boy through lush berries. HarperCollins, 1985.

17 Kings and 42 Elephants by Margaret Mahy. Take a royal romp through a tongue-twisting tropical paradise. Dial, 1972.

Some Things Go Together by Charlotte Zolotow. Colorful illustrations accompany couplets describing things that go together naturally such as "sand with sea" and especially "you with me." HarperCollins, 1987.

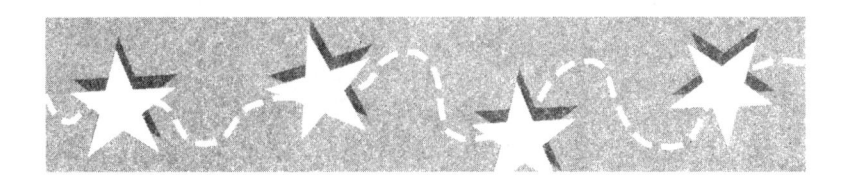

The Eency Weency Spider

1. The een-cy, ween-cy spi-der went up the wa-ter spout,
6. Down came the rain and washed the spi-der out
10. Out came the sun and dried up all the rain, and the
14. een-cy, ween-cy spi-der went up the spout a-gain.

Music Expansion

Ask children how they think the spider would move. Encourage them to use the movements as they sing the song.

Change the words *the eency weency spider* to *the great big daddy spider*, *the medium mommy spider*, or *the tiny baby spider*. Ask children what kind of voice each type of spider would use and how they could show that size spider moving. Then invite children to sing the new verses using daddy, mommy, and baby voices and movements.

Encourage children to vary the tempo as they sing the song. Then invite them to pretend to be spiders and move to the various tempos.

Themes

Counting/Numbers
Cultures
Folklore and Tales
Insects
Position Words
Spiders

Featured Book

Anansi the Spider: a tale from the Ashanti adapted by Gerald McDermott

Curriculum Integration

Choose activities from the following curriculum areas that fit your teaching style and the needs and interests of the children.

Science

Take children outside to look for spiders. When one is located, invite children to observe it and its surroundings. Carefully catch the spider and place it in a large jar with holes punched in the lid or a screen or cloth covering. Add leaves, sticks, or other materials from the surrounding area. Place the jar in the science area and encourage children to observe the spider. Provide a journal for the children to record their observations. After several days, return the spider to its original surroundings.

Place water, big blocks, and toy spiders in the water table or a large tub. Have children "wash the spider out." Encourage them to talk about what they think would happen to a spider in a rainstorm and in the sunshine.

Explain that most spiders have eight eyes. Place multifaceted viewers (available at most toy stores) in the science area. Invite children to look through them and talk about what surroundings must look like from a spider's point of view.

Invite children to look at a dead spider using a microscope or magnifying glass and talk about what they see.

Math

Remind children that insects have six legs but spiders have eight legs and eight eyes. Invite children to sort blocks or counters into sets of eight.

Invite children to make spider games. Provide each child with a 6" x 6" piece of oak tag. Have children draw spider bodies on the oak tag. Then have each child cut eight narrow strips from black construction paper for legs.

Arrange children in pairs or groups of three or four to play the game. Provide each pair or group with a die or number cards with from one to six dots on them. Have children take turns rolling the die or drawing cards. Encourage children to count the dots on the die or card. Then have them add that number of legs to their spiders. The first child in each pair or group to complete an eight-legged spider wins.

Provide a flannel board and a felt spider and down spout. Ask children where else the spider might have gone besides up and down. Encourage children to position the spider in relation to the down spout as they use the position word.

Art

Provide children with clay and suggest that they make spiders. They might wish to use toothpicks for legs or for making details on the clay.

Read *Anansi the Spider: a tale from the Ashanti*. Then display the illustrations where the six sons are introduced. Count the legs on one of the spiders and talk about the shapes Mr. McDermott used in the illustrations. Place various colors of construction paper, scissors, and glue in the art area. Have children create their own spiders. When the spiders are completed, attach them to strings and hang them from the ceiling.

Reading/Writing

Read *Anansi the Spider*. Ask children what special quality each son has. Then ask them to name something special about themselves. Write each response on the bottom of a sheet of drawing paper. Have children draw pictures of themselves that show their special traits.

Read the last ten pages of *Anansi the Spider*. Ask children what they think the ball of light is. Then explain that this is an African folktale that tells how the moon came to be. Invite children to make up stories which explain how something came to be. Have them write or dictate the stories and illustrate them. Or have them write a class story.

Social Studies

Display a world map and point out Africa and Ghana. Explain that this is the home of the Ashanti people. Have children find their country on the map. Have children compare the sizes of their country and Ghana. Then provide children with some of the information from the prologue.

Visit the library and look for books about spiders and insects or books about African or other folktales.

Related Literature

Anansi the Spider: a tale from the Ashanti adapted by Gerald McDermott. Anansi, the spider hero of African folklore, is saved by the combined talents of his six sons. Holt, 1972.

Ashanti to Zulu: African Traditions by Margaret Musgrove. This descriptive alphabet book focuses on customs of African tribes. Dial, 1976.

The Eency Weency Spider by Joanne Oppenheim. A popular children's song is retold and expanded to include other nursery rhymes. Bantam, 1991.

Spider by Michael Chinery. The physical characteristics and the life cycle of the spider are explored. Troll, 1991.

Spiders by Kate Petty. This book explains spiders and their habits in simple language children can understand. Watts, 1990.

The Farmer in the Dell

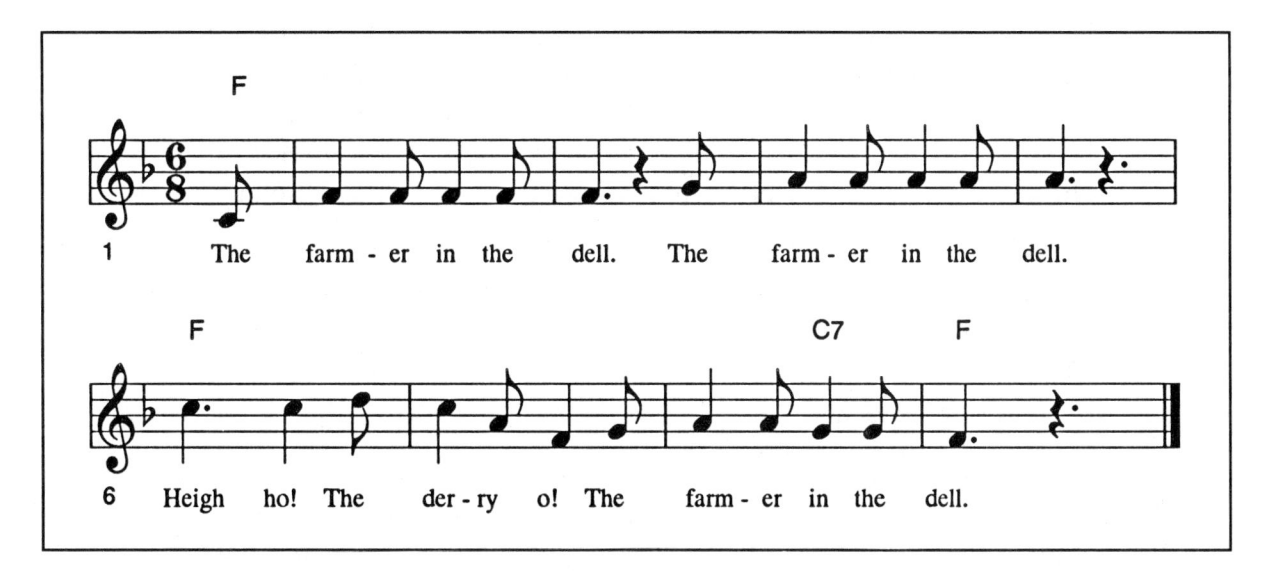

1 The farmer in the dell. The farmer in the dell.
6 Heigh ho! The derry o! The farmer in the dell.

Additional verses

The farmer takes the wife . . .

The wife takes the child . . .

The child takes the nurse . . .

The nurse takes the dog . . .

The dog takes the cat . . .

The cat takes the rat . . .

The rat takes the cheese . . .

The cheese stands alone . . .

Music Expansion

Provide props to enhance this song. For example, have a straw hat for the farmer, an apron for the wife, and a white coat or cap for the nurse. Have children wear or hold props as they sing.

Invite children to sing the song using other items that might be found on a farm such as a tractor, hay, corn, or pig.

Ask one child to be the farmer. Have the other children form a circle around the farmer. As the first verse is sung, have the farmer choose a child from the circle to be the wife and stand inside the circle also. As the second verse is sung, the wife chooses someone from the circle to be the child. Continue in this manner until the last verse. Then, as the last verse is sung, have everyone but the cheese return to the circle. The cheese can then become the farmer for the next round of singing.

Invite the class to make up new words for the song according to a theme. For example, if the theme is the zoo, the first verse might be "The zookeeper in the zoo." Encourage children to make verses about things associated with a zoo. If the theme is dinosaurs, the first verse might be "The dinosaurs long ago."

Use the song to introduce children to each other. The song could be sung at the beginning of the school year or when a new child joins the class. Substitute children's names for characters in the original song. An example of the song might be

> The children in our class.
> The children in our class.
> Heigh, ho! We all are friends.
> The children in our class.
>
> Elliott takes Mary . . .

Themes

Animals
Community Helpers
Family
Farms
Food/Nutrition
Growing Things
Health

Featured Book

The Farmer by Rosalinda Kightley

Curriculum Integration

Choose activities from the following curriculum areas that fit your teaching style and the needs and interests of the children.

Science

Invite children to make butter. Provide each child with a clean baby-food jar. Have each child measure 1/4 cup heavy cream, add it to a jar, and replace the lid. Play some lively music and encourage children to shake the jar to the music. It will take approximately ten minutes for the cream to turn to butter. Help children pour the buttermilk into glasses. Encourage them to taste it. If desired, have each child add a pinch of salt to the butter and beat it with a spoon. Serve the butter with crackers for a snack.

Provide children with a large tub, planter box, or a small plot of ground outside. Encourage children to work soil with shovels or trowels. Then invite them to plant seeds and care for a garden. (Plants such as lettuce and peas that don't need much root depth do best in tubs and planters.) Have children keep a farm journal to record what was done in the garden and how the garden changes.

Make a farm discovery table in the science area. Provide farm magazines, toy farm vehicles, plastic animals, hay, corn, wool, a hard-boiled egg, and other farm-related items. Encourage children to handle the items, ask questions about farms, and talk about what they know of farms.

Math

Make a graph of children's favorite farm animals. Help children come to conclusions by asking questions about the graph. Which animal was the favorite? Which was the least favorite?

Have children sort pictures of animals according to whether or not they can be found on farms.

Show children pictures of farm products. Invite children to classify the pictures by their origin. Help them decide if the items came from plants or animals.

Art

Provide boxes for children to make into barns. Provide art materials such as paints, brushes, crayons, markers, straw, construction paper, glue, and scissors. Also provide a variety of pictures of barns so children can see examples of features they may want to include on their barns.

Invite children to make buttermilk and chalk pictures. Have children use fat paintbrushes to lightly cover drawing paper with buttermilk. Then encourage children to use colored chalk to draw farm scenes. When the buttermilk dries, the chalk will not rub off easily.

Provide children with old magazines and invite them to make a "meal" of foods that come from a farm. Ask children to cut out pictures of foods that they think come from farms and glue them to paper plates.

Reading/Writing

Read *The Farmer*. Talk about how the family works together on the farm. Make a list of the chores done by family members. Then ask children how they help at home. Have them draw pictures of themselves doing chores or helping around the house. When the pictures are finished, suggest that each child write or dictate something about the picture.

Ask children to recite nursery rhymes about the farm or growing things. Examples include "Little Boy Blue" or "Mistress Mary." Write the lines of the rhymes on sentence strips. Draw or glue cutout pictures to represent each sentence or phrase on each strip. Help children sequence the strips as they recite the rhymes. Place the strips in the language area and encourage each child to sequence the strips.

Social Studies

Read *The Farmer* aloud to children. Display the illustration showing the farmer's market selling farm products. Explain that farmers raise the crops and then they sell the products directly to people or to a grocery store. Then visit a farmer's market or a grocery store.

Arrange a field trip to a nearby farm. Encourage children to ask questions about the farm, equipment, crops, and animals.

Talk about how farm goods get to market. Change the words to "The Farmer in the Dell" to show what a farmer does with his crops. An example of some verses might be

The farmer's in the field . . .

The farmer picks the corn . . .

He puts it in a truck . . .

He takes it to the store . . .

Related Literature

The Farmer by Rosalinda Kightley. In rhyming text, this story follows a busy farmer as he milks cows, plows fields, and oils his tractor. Macmillan, 1987.

Good Morning, Chick by Mirra Ginsburg. With his mother, a little chick starts to explore the world around him. William Morrow, 1980.

Hide-and-Seek on the Farm by Laura Damon. As the barnyard animals play hide-and-seek, it's fun to join in by helping to find them. Troll, 1987.

The Milk Makers by Gail Gibbons. The book describes the production and processing of milk from the time a cow grazes until the milk reaches the table. Macmillan, 1985.

Rosie's Walk by Pat Hutchins. Rosie the hen goes out for a walk around the barnyard and unknowingly outwits a fox. Macmillan, 1971.

Three Ducks Went Wandering by Ron Roy. Blind luck protects three little ducks when they venture out of the barnyard. Houghton Mifflin, 1988.

He's Got the Whole World

[Musical notation with lyrics:]

He's got the whole world in His hands. He's got the whole world in His hands. He's got the whole world in His hands. He's got the whole world in His hands.

Additional verses

He's got you and me brother in His hands.
He's got you and me sister in His hands.
He's got you and me brother in His hands.
He's got the whole world in His hands.

Repeat the first verse.

He's got the little tiny babies . . .

Repeat the first verse.

(Change the word *He's* to the word *We've* and the word *His* to the word *our*, if desired.)

56

Music Expansion

For a theme on ecology, change the words of the first verse to "We've got the whole world in our hands." The following verses could reflect things found in the environment. Some examples of these verses might include

We've got the butterflies and birds in our hands . . .

We've got the trees and the flowers in our hands . . .

Invite someone who knows sign language to come in and teach children the signs for this song. Often volunteers can be found by contacting a local college or university, the public library, a school, or a church.

Themes

Cultures
Ecology
Friends
Self-Awareness

Featured Book

People by Peter Spier

Curriculum Integration

Choose activities from the following curriculum areas that fit your teaching style and the needs and interests of the children.

Science

Read the first seven pages of *People*. Invite children to make a list of what they have in common with each other. For instance, they all have two eyes, one nose, and hair. Then have them list some of the differences. For example, some children have blond hair, and others have black. Some children have blue eyes, and some have brown eyes. Discuss how these differences make each child special and unlike anyone else.

Place magnifying glasses in the science area. Invite children to use the magnifying glasses to examine their hands and the hands of other classmates. Suggest they look for similarities and differences. Then offer children an ink pad and paper. Have them press their thumbs and fingers on the ink pad and then onto the paper. Encourage them to view the fingerprints through the magnifying glasses and notice any differences.

Point out that all people share one planet and many people try to take care of it by saving resources. Ask children to describe things they do at home to save resources. Some children may talk about recycling. Others may mention shutting off lights when they're not in a room. Still others might talk about saving water by not watering the lawn. Write the responses on chart paper and post it in the science area.

Math

Encourage children to group themselves by hair color, eye color, or another characteristic. Make a graph for each characteristic. Help children notice that not all characteristics are shared by the same children. For example, two children may have the same color hair but not the same color eyes.

Invite children to line up according to height. The children might do this as an entire group, or each child might take a turn arranging the rest of the children.

Social Studies

Plan a clean-up day and pick up trash around the school. Provide bags and invite children to clean up trash around the school, playground, or neighborhood. They could then recycle the trash into a mural. (See Art.)

Art

Provide children with magazines and invite them to make people collages. Ask them to cut out pictures of people and glue the pictures to sheets of construction paper. Encourage children to notice similarities and differences of the people in the collage.

Invite children to draw or paint pictures of where they think the best place in the whole world might be. They might draw pictures of their homes, forests, mountains, farms, or other locations. When the pictures are finished, ask children to write or dictate something about their pictures.

Have children make a trash mural using some of the trash they found during their clean-up day. (See Social Studies.) Then encourage children to write or dictate slogans on the mural paper about environmental responsibility. Hang the mural in a prominent place in the school.

Reading/Writing

Read *People*. Pause frequently so children can talk about the messages in the text or in the pictures.

Help children trace their hands on paper. Then have them write or dictate what they can do to take care of the earth.

Draw and cut out a giant hand outline. Ask children to draw, write, or dictate things that can go in the big hand.

Related Literature

All Kinds, Who Cares About Race and Colour by Pam Adams. The focus of this book is to create in children an understanding of the basic value and worth of people of different races and colors. Child's Play, 1990.

Farewell to Shady Glade by Bill Peet. Sixteen tenants of a tree house are faced with a plight common to our own century—progress. Houghton Mifflin, 1966.

The Lorax by Dr. Seuss. The Once-ler describes the results of the local pollution problem. Random, 1971.

People by Peter Spier. Peter Spier shows—through words and pictures—how exciting the variety of people really is and how sad the world would be if we were all the same. Doubleday, 1980.

Rain Forest by Helen Cowcher. The rain forest, full of lush vegetation and exotic animals, is a peaceful place until people and machines threaten to destroy it. Farrar, Straus, and Giroux, 1988.

Head, Shoulders, Knees, and Toes

1. Head and shoul-ders, knees and toes, knees and toes. Head and shoul-ders, knees and

4. toes, knees and toes. Eyes and ears and mouth and nose,

7. Head and shoul-ders, knees and toes, knees and toes. toes, knees and toes.

Music Expansion

Invite children to touch places on their bodies as the song is sung. Vary the tempo. Sing the song several times, singing faster each time.

Encourage children to think of other parts of the body such as arms, eyes, or hips that they could sing about.

This song is wonderful for teaching the names of the parts of the body not only in English, but in foreign languages as well. If any children come from a bilingual home environment, invite them or a family member to teach the vocabulary. Or you could use the Spanish suggestions on the next page.

head	shoulder	knee	toe	foot
cabeza	hombro	rodilla	dedo	pie
nose	eye	ear	neck	cheek
nariz	ojo	oído	cuello	mejilla
teeth	elbow	arm	chin	skin
diente	codo	brazo	barba	piel

As children sing, leave out the word for one body part while continuing to point to that part. For example:

_____ and shoulders, knees and toes . . .

_____ and _____, knees and toes . . .

Themes
Body
Health
Self-Awareness

Featured Book
Here Are My Hands by Bill Martin Jr. and John Archambault

Curriculum Integration
Choose activities from the following curriculum areas that fit your teaching style and the needs and interests of the children.

Science
Put cutouts of parts of the body on the flannel board and invite children to build a person.

Ask children which animals have shoulders, knees, and toes. Make a list of the animals the children name on chart paper. Then invite children to look through old magazines for pictures of the animals to glue next to their names.

Read *Here Are My Hands*. Invite children to talk about how a person takes care of his or her body. Point out that the children in the book are keeping clean. Ask them what else is needed to have a healthy body.

Math

Invite children to count the number of heads, shoulders, knees, or toes in the room. Some children may want to count by ones, twos, or fives.

Read *Here Are My Hands*. Ask children to recall some of the parts of the body mentioned in the book. Write the names of the parts across the top of chart paper. Then encourage children to name all the things the body part can do. List these below the body part. When the chart is finished, invite children to estimate how many things are in each column, which column has the most, and which has the fewest. Then have children count the number in each column.

Art

Invite children to make a hands and toes painting. Place a long sheet of butcher paper on the floor. Cover a cookie sheet with a thin layer of tempera paint and put it at one end of the paper. (Have several colors available.) Have barefooted children tiptoe first onto the cookie sheet and then across the paper. At the end of the paper have a small tub of water in which children can wash their feet. Then have the children press their hands in the paint and make handprints across the paper.

Suggest children make body puzzles. Have children work in pairs. Have one child lie on a sheet of butcher paper while the other child traces around the first with a crayon. Then have them switch places. Encourage each child to decorate the tracing to look like himself or herself and cut it out. Help children cut the tracings into five to ten pieces for a body puzzle.

Reading/Writing

Read *Here Are My Hands* and invite children to make their own books. Offer children several sheets of drawing paper and ask them to draw different parts of the body. Below the drawings, suggest children write or dictate something about the part. For example, one child might draw his or her hair and then tell what color it is and that it keeps the head warm. When the pages for the books are completed, encourage children to decorate a construction paper cover and then assemble the cover and pages into a book. Invite volunteers to read their books to the class.

Have children brainstorm all the parts of the body they can possibly think of while you write the words on chart paper. Invite children to use these words to sing the song again while pointing to the various parts.

Social Studies

Look at the differences and similarities in people's features such as skin color and hair type. Talk about how these traits help make each person a unique individual.

Arrange a visit to a zoo and ask children to look for animals that have shoulders. (Most children will only see primates as having shoulders.)

Invite a doctor, nurse, or nutritionist to visit the classroom. Suggest that the guest talk with children about what they can do to have a healthy body.

Related Literature

The Biggest Nose by Kathy Caple. Eleanor the elephant is self-conscious about her large nose, but she overcomes her sensitivity when she realizes Betty the hippo has the biggest mouth. Houghton Mifflin, 1985.

Gregory, the Terrible Eater by Mitchell Sharmat. No junk food for Gregory Goat—he'll eat fruits and vegetables. Macmillan, 1980.

Here Are My Hands by Bill Martin, Jr. and John Archambault. The owners of human bodies celebrate by pointing out various parts and mentioning their functions, from "hands are for catching" to the "skin that bundles me in." Holt, 1985.

People by Peter Spier. Peter Spier shows—through words and pictures—how exciting the variety of people really is, and how sad the world would be if we were all the same. Doubleday, 1980.

Your Skin and Mine by Paul Showers. From freckles to fingerprints to follicles, learn all about skin—what it is and how it protects you. HarperCollins, 1965.

Hickety Tickety Bumblebee

(Sheet music in 3/4 time, key of C)

1. Hick-e-ty, tick-e-ty bum-ble-bee. Can
5. you sing your name to me?
9. Ja——-mie, Ja——-mie.

Music Expansion

Invite children to form a circle. Explain that they are the beehive. Then choose one child to stand in the center. Have children making the beehive move in one direction around the child in the middle and stop on "Can you sing your name to me?" After singing his or her name, the child in the middle chooses another child to exchange places and be next "in the beehive."

Ask children to form a circle and pretend to be flowers. Invite one child to stand in the center of the circle and pretend to be a bee. Invite the bee to choose a flower and sing or say its name. That child then becomes the bee.

If a child is too shy to say or sing his or her name, change the words to "everyone sing his/her name to me."

Themes

Counting/Numbers
Growing Things
Insects

Featured Book

The Icky Bug Counting Book by Jerry Pallotta

Curriculum Integration

Choose activities from the following curriculum areas that fit your teaching style and the needs and interests of the children.

Science

Help children set up a garden area inside or outside. For an indoor garden, offer children potting soil, cups or a large tub, hand gardening tools, and flower seeds. For an outdoor garden, provide a sunny plot, gardening tools, and flower seeds. Invite children to work the soil, plant the seeds, and then water the soil. Have children discuss what plants need to help them grow. Then encourage children to tend the gardens. Suggest they record their observations of the plant growth in a science journal by drawing pictures and writing or dictating.

Show pictures of different types of bees. Ask children why they think bees like flowers. Talk about how bees collect pollen and nectar from flowers and turn it into honey. Set out some fresh garden flowers, such as daisies, and dark construction paper. Invite each child to hold a flower over a sheet of construction paper and shake or rub the flower's center. Have children use magnifying glasses to look at the flecks of pollen.

Math

Make flowers for the flannel board. Cut out centers and petals separately. Place a center on the flannel board and place some petals around it. Have children count the number of petals on the flower. Next ask a child to place a specific number of petals on each center. Or invite children to roll dice, count the spots, and place that number of petals on the flower center. Invite children to work in pairs with the flowers.

Read *The Icky Bug Counting Book*. Talk about zero. If necessary, explain that zero is the same as nothing. Then have children count the bugs on each page as you read.

Social Studies

Visit a grocery store or a health food store. Purchase a honeycomb and encourage children to examine it with a magnifying glass before and after they eat the honey.

Visit an apiary or invite a beekeeper to visit the class. Ask the beekeeper to show and explain the equipment he or she uses and wears. Encourage children to ask questions about bees and beekeeping.

Visit a nursery and find out which flowers attract insects. If possible, purchase some flower plants and plant them outside the school. Encourage children to observe any insects around the flowers and tell the class what they have seen.

Art

Invite children to listen to a recording of "The Flight of the Bumblebee" by Rimsky-Korsakov. Then offer children paper and crayons and suggest they draw the bumblebee's flight as they listen to the recording again.

After serving honey from a honeycomb (see Social Studies), invite children to take turns dipping the honeycomb into tempera paint and making prints on their papers. Then suggest that each child dip a thumb in the paint and make thumbprints around the honeycomb print. Have children decorate the thumbprints as bees. Display the pictures on a wall or bulletin board.

Reading/Writing

Read *The Icky Bug Counting Book*. Ask children which bugs they found interesting. Also have them discuss how they think each bug got its name.

Ask children what they think a Hickety Tickety Bumblebee is. What does it look like? What does it do all day? Invite children to write or dictate their ideas on paper and illustrate them. Bind the papers together to make a Hickety Tickety Bumblebee book.

Related Literature

Ant Cities by Arthur Dorros. The book explains how ants live and work together to build and maintain their cities. HarperCollins, 1988.

The Flower Alphabet Book by Jerry Pallotta. An alphabet book of flowers, including fun facts and information about flowers of all kinds. Charlesbridge, 1989.

The Icky Bug Counting Book by Jerry Pallotta. This book not only introduces the numbers 1 through 26 but also offers a fascinating exploration of bugs of all kinds. A secret—the bugs are listed alphabetically when read from 26 through 1. Charlesbridge, 1992.

Planting a Rainbow by Lois Ehlert. Bold and exuberant pictures show the planting of a family garden. Bulbs, seeds, and seedlings grow into a brilliant rainbow of colorful flowers that are picked and carried home. And next year, a rainbow can grow all over again. Harcourt, 1988.

A Seed Is a Promise by Claire Merrill. A science book for young readers that explores the fascinating world of seeds, how they are made, and how they make new plants. Scholastic, 1990.

Hickory Dickory Dock

[Sheet music in 6/8 time, key of C]

1. Hick-o-ry dick-o-ry dock. The mouse ran up the
4. clock. The clock struck one, the mouse ran down.
7. Hick-o-ry dick-o-ry dock.

Additional verses

. . . The clock struck two,
The mouse said, "Boo!" . . .

. . . The clock struck three,
The mouse said, "Whee-e-e!" . . .

. . . The clock struck four,
The mouse said, "No more!" . . .

Music Expansion

Offer children a variety of instruments. These might include rhythm sticks for the sound of the clock ticking, a slide whistle for the mouse running up or down, and a triangle for the clock sounding one. Or after demonstrating each instrument, invite children to choose which instrument should represent each sound.

Ask children what other animals might run up the clock. What might happen if an elephant runs up the clock? What ways would some of the animals move up the clock? For example, an elephant would trudge and a duck would waddle. Invite children to sing the song again using new animals and movements.

Themes

Animals
Counting/Numbers
Nursery Rhymes
Position Words
Time

Featured Book

Nicola Bayley's Book of Nursery Rhymes by Nicola Bayley

Curriculum Integration

Choose activities from the following curriculum areas that fit your teaching style and the needs and interests of the children.

Science

Set up a time discovery table. Provide various timepieces such as clocks, oven timers, egg timers, hourglasses, and watches. If possible, have several old clocks that children can take apart and see all the pieces that make them run. Point out how the hands on a clock move or the sand passes through the top to the bottom of an hourglass just as time moves. If a true hourglass is available, make marks on it to indicate lunchtime, playtime, or some other activity time.

Ask children how they think people knew what time it was before clocks were invented. How would people know when to get up, eat lunch, or go to bed?

Keep a mouse as a class pet. Invite children to take turns caring for it. Encourage them to keep a journal of their observations.

Math

Invite children to sing the song again. Have children clap their hands or play rhythm sticks the number of times the clock strikes.

Make clocks and mice for the flannel board. Model for children how to place a mouse and clock on a flannel board and describe their relationship. For example, place the mouse under the clock and say, "The mouse is under the clock." Invite children to place mice and clocks on the flannel board and, using position words, describe where the mice are. Suggest children work in pairs or small groups.

Make a lotto game of timepieces. Draw or cut out pictures of a variety of different timepieces. You will need to draw or cut out two identical pictures of each timepiece. Glue one set of pictures to a game board. Glue the other set of pictures to individual cards. Invite children to match picture cards to the game board.

Art

Invite children to make mouse masks. Provide paper plates, construction paper and fabric scraps, markers, pipe cleaners, scissors, and glue. Help children cut holes in paper plates for eyes. Then suggest they use the materials to create mice faces. When the masks are completed, help children attach tie strings to the sides of their masks. Invite children to wear the masks as they sing and act out the song.

Read *Nicola Bayley's Book of Nursery Rhymes*. Provide a variety of art materials and ask children to illustrate one of their favorite nursery rhymes from the book or other rhymes they might know. Encourage volunteers to show their illustrations and recite the rhymes to the class.

Reading/Writing

Invite children to write or dictate a story about their favorite time of day.

Read *Nicola Bayley's Book of Nursery Rhymes*. Ask children what they think happens after each nursery rhyme ends. What happens to the children in the shoe the next day? Where does the crooked little man go when he walks his crooked mile? What happens to the spider and Miss Muffet? Have children write or dictate their new nursery rhyme endings.

Social Studies

Ask children to think of things that go up and down. Make a list on chart paper and hang it on a wall. Then invite children to go on a walk in the neighborhood. Encourage them to look for things that go up and down. When they return, have them add the new things to the list. Suggest they look at home for things that move up and down and add those to the list as well.

Related Literature

The Berenstain Bears' Nursery Tales by Stan and Jan Berenstain. The delightful bear family takes the reader on a journey into the world of nursery rhymes. Random, 1973.

Chinese Mother Goose Rhymes selected and edited by Robert Wyndham. This collection of nursery rhymes translated from Chinese includes some on ladybugs, kites, and bumps on the head. The rhymes are also presented in Chinese characters. Sandcastle, 1989.

Each Peach Pear Plum by Janet and Allan Ahlberg. An enticing "I Spy" rhyme book that delights readers with nursery-rhyme and fairy-tale characters hidden in playful drawings. Scholastic, 1986.

Nicola Bayley's Book of Nursery Rhymes by Nicola Bayley. This is a collection of 22 favorite Mother Goose nursery rhymes. Knopf, 1975.

Where Are You Going, Little Mouse? by Robert Kraus. When it starts to get dark, Little Mouse starts to have second thoughts about running away from home and soon decides that home wasn't such a bad place after all. Greenwillow, 1986.

If You're Happy and You Know It

1 If you're hap-py and you know it, clap your hands. [clap] [clap] If you're
4 hap-py and you know it, clap your hands. [clap] [clap] If you're
6 hap-py and you know it, then your face will sure-ly show it. If you're
8 hap-py and you know it, clap your hands. [clap] [clap]

Additional verses

. . . stomp your feet . . .

. . . nod your head . . .

. . . shout hooray . . .

. . . do all four . . .

Music Expansion

Encourage children to do the actions indicated by the song's words.

Talk about other emotions—sad, happy, angry, surprised. Ask children to make faces showing these emotions. How would their voices sound? Invite children to use some of these ideas in the song. Examples might include "If you're sad and you know it, cry boo-hoo" or "If you're mad and you know it, stomp your feet."

Have children discuss other ways to feel. What movements and sounds could be used to show a person is hungry, tired, or silly?

Invite children to use instruments in the song. For example, "If you're happy and you know it, play your drum . . . If you're happy and you know it, then your instrument will show it. If you're happy and you know it, play your drum."

Themes

Emotions/Feelings
Self-Awareness

Featured Book

the temper tantrum book by Edna Mitchell Preston

Curriculum Integration

Choose activities from the following curriculum areas that fit your teaching style and the needs and interests of the children.

Science

Encourage children to measure the ingredients and observe changes as they make feelings cookies from the recipe on the next page. Offer children raisins and string licorice to use for faces that are happy, sad, angry, surprised, or another emotion.

Feelings Sugar Cookies

Ingredients

2/3 cup shortening
3/4 cup sugar
1 teaspoon vanilla
1 egg
4 teaspoons milk
2 cups flour
1 1/2 teaspoons baking powder
1/4 teaspoon salt

Utensils

measuring cups
measuring spoons
bowl
mixer
rolling pin
round cookie cutter
cookie sheet

Cream shortening, sugar, and vanilla. Add egg and beat till light and fluffy. Stir in milk. Slowly add dry ingredients into creamed mixture. Chill for one hour.

Roll dough on a floured surface to about 1/8" thickness. Cut with round cookie cutter and place circles on a greased cookie sheet. Add faces to the cookies. Bake at 375°F for 6 to 9 minutes. Cool slightly before removing from sheet. Makes about 4 dozen.

Tape-record sounds that can be associated with feelings such as crying, laughing, and growling. Play the tape and ask children to identify the feelings they think the sounds are associated with.

Math

Make emotion faces for the flannel board. Place three faces showing the same emotion and one face showing a different emotion on the flannel board. Ask children to pick the one that is different. Or make patterns with the faces and ask children to complete the pattern. For example, place a happy face, sad face, happy face, and a sad face on the flannel board. Ask children to add the face that comes next.

Art

Invite children to cut out magazine pictures of people showing different feelings. Have them glue the pictures onto sheets of paper and write or dictate stories about why they think the people in the pictures might have those feelings.

Explain that music and art often reflect the way people are feeling. Play some happy-sounding music and ask children what they think of when they hear the music. Do the same with sad-sounding music and angry-sounding music. (Selections from classical music work well.) Then invite children to listen to the music again, choose markers or crayons, and create designs that show the feelings.

Reading/Writing

Read *the temper tantrum book*. Ask children to talk about the words in the book that describe the animals' feelings. Then invite children to create a class book about emotions. Offer children paper and crayons and ask them to draw pictures of themselves showing different emotions. Then have them explain what would make them feel each emotion and how that emotion would make them act. Encourage them to use words to describe the feelings as they write or dictate their descriptions.

I feel happy when . . . and feeling happy makes me . . .

I feel sad when . . . and feeling sad makes me . . .

Social Studies

Have children plan a Grandparents' Day celebration. Encourage each child to invite a grandparent or other older adult to visit the class. Help children plan refreshments, decorations, and entertainment. Some of the adults might read to the children.

Plan a happiness party for a retirement or nursing home or a senior-citizen center. Have children make pictures to give to the older people and practice singing songs such as "If You're Happy and You Know It." Sharing happiness with the seniors could become a regular visit for the children.

Related Literature

Alexander and the Terrible, Horrible, No Good, Very Bad Day by Judith Viorst. From waking up with gum in his hair to having lima beans for supper, Alexander finds there are days when nothing goes right. Atheneum, 1987.

Feelings by Aliki. Pictures, dialogues, poems, and stories portray various emotions we all feel: jealousy, sadness, fear, anger, joy, love, and others. Morrow, 1986.

The Hating Book by Charlotte Zolotow. An engaging story of the ups and downs of a friendship where hate looms large then happily vanishes when the reason for it is understood. HarperCollins, 1989.

The Quarreling Book by Charlotte Zolotow. Anger is passed along from person to person until a little dog starts a chain of happiness that reverses the trend. HarperCollins, 1953.

the temper tantrum book by Edna Mitchell Preston. Stomping, howling, squealing, and frowning young animals express their anger at situations that frustrate and annoy many small children. Penguin, 1963.

Jack and Jill

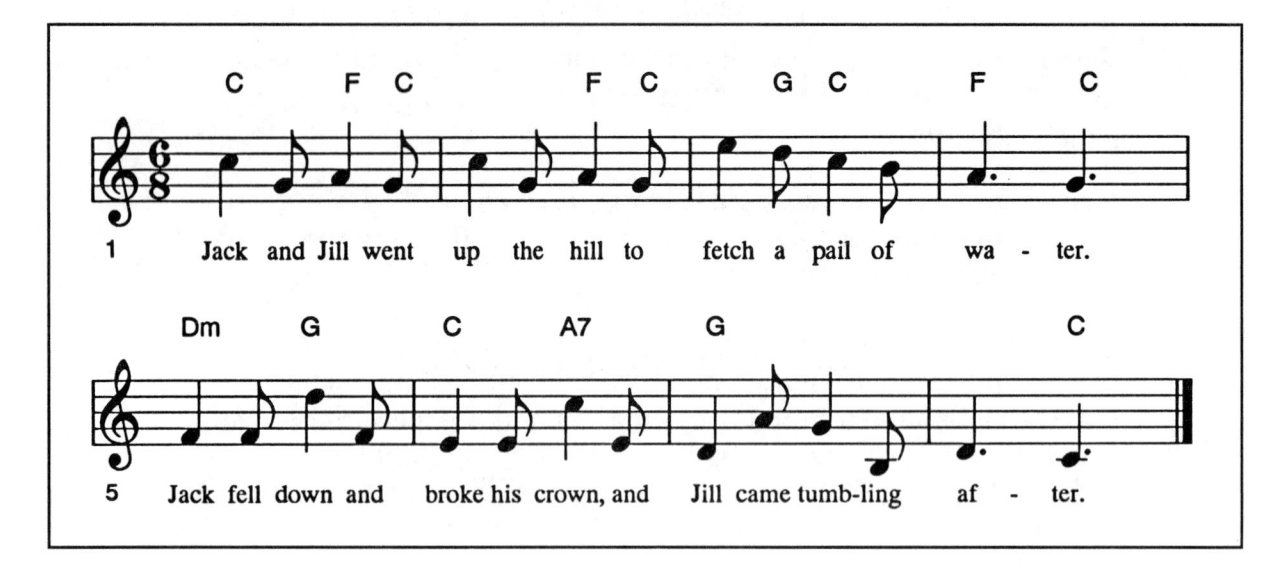

[Musical notation with chords C, F, C, F, C, G, C, F, C for first line: "Jack and Jill went up the hill to fetch a pail of water."]

[Second line chords Dm, G, C, A7, G, C: "Jack fell down and broke his crown, and Jill came tumbling after."]

Music Expansion

Invite children to act out the song. Instead of Jack and Jill, use names of two of the children and suggest that they act out the song. Then have those two children pick two more children to act out the song.

Ask children to suggest places where Jack and Jill might go instead of going up the hill. Have them make up new words for the song. An example might be

> Jack and Jill went down the street
> To find their friend named Tommy.
> Tom came out and they did pout
> 'Cause he wouldn't share his salami!

(Note: The children's examples don't need to rhyme.)

Provide instruments for children to create sound effects. They might use tone bells in graduated steps for going up the hill, a slide whistle for falling down, a cymbal crash for breaking Jack's crown, and bells for Jill tumbling after.

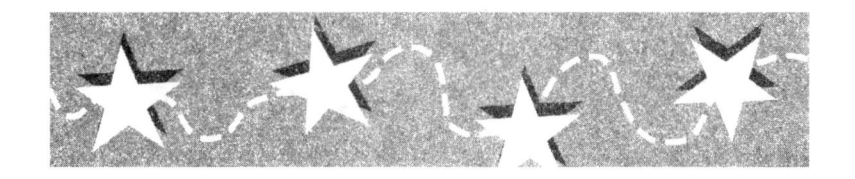

Themes

Nursery Rhymes
Position Words
Simple Machines

Featured Book

Tikki Tikki Tembo retold by Arlene Mosel

Curriculum Integration

Choose activities from the following curriculum areas that fit your teaching style and the needs and interests of the children.

Science

Read *Tikki Tikki Tembo*. Help children notice that at the top of the well there is a rope attached to a pulley. Rig up a pulley system with a pail attached. You might be able to hang a small pulley from a hook in the ceiling or doorway or from a tree outside. Provide another identical pail and blocks. Ask children to fill the pail with blocks and try to lift it. What happens? Then have children transfer the blocks to the pail attached to the pulley rope. Have them pull on the rope to raise the pail. Encourage children to explain what happened using words such as *heavy, light, easier,* and *harder.*

Place different sizes of containers and pails in a water table. Invite children to pour water between different sizes of containers and to talk about their observations. Encourage them to use words such as *smaller, larger, more,* and *less.*

Encourage children to build hills or slanted surfaces (inclined planes) using blocks and wooden planks. Then invite children to experiment by rolling items down the hills. They might use toy cars, marbles, other blocks, or items found in the classroom. Suggest children try moving the items up the hills. Ask questions such as "Did the items move better down or up the hills? Why?" Encourage children to talk about their observations.

Math

Display different sizes of containers or small pails. Invite children to put them in order according to size. Then ask children which they think will hold more. Which will hold less? Provide buttons, stones, or small blocks and encourage children to fill the containers and compare the amounts in each.

Provide a variety of sorting materials and pails. Invite children to sort the items into the pails and discuss how they sorted the items.

Art

Have children take pails of water and different sizes of brushes outside and then "paint" pictures and designs on the sidewalk or driveway.

Offer clay to children and suggest they make hills and figures of Jack and Jill. Encourage them to act out the nursery rhyme with the clay props.

Reading/Writing

Read *Tikki Tikki Tembo*. Ask children how the song about Jack and Jill and the story are alike and different.

Invite children to write a group story about what happened to Jack and Jill after they fell down the hill. Have children take turns creating sentences or phrases. Write their responses on a large sheet of chart paper. Encourage children to continue until they decide the story is finished. (Read the story at intervals to remind children what has already been dictated.) Read the final story to them. Have children illustrate their story on separate sheets of paper. Post the story in a prominent place with the illustrations around it.

Social Studies

If there is a hill nearby, invite children to walk up and then down the hill. Encourage them to talk about the differences in going up and going down. Ask them to think of other ways to go up or down the hill. Invite them to demonstrate their ideas.

If possible, arrange to visit a farm or other place that has an old-fashioned well. Ask children why they think Jack and Jill and Tikki Tikki Tembo had to get water from a well. Have children talk about where they think their water comes from.

Related Literature

Mother Goose on the Rio Grande by Frances Alexander. Featuring lively rhythms and charming drawings of children and animals, this book brings to youngsters the interplay of language and culture found in Mexico and the American Southwest. National Textbook Company, 1983.

The Mother Goose Treasury by Raymond Briggs. A comprehensive anthology of 408 rhymes and 897 illustrations that includes all the best-loved verses as well as many unfamiliar ones. Dell, 1986.

over, under & through by Tana Hoban. Photographs demonstrate the spatial concepts expressed in twelve words such as *around*, *between*, *against*, and *behind*. Atheneum, 1973.

Simple Machines by Rae Bains. This book describes six simple machines—pulley, lever, wheel, inclined plane, wedge, and screw—upon which all other machines are based. Troll, 1985.

Tikki Tikki Tembo retold by Arlene Mosel. A charming Chinese folktale about a boy named Chang and his brother, whose long name causes problems when he falls into a well. Holt, 1989.

Johnny Hammers

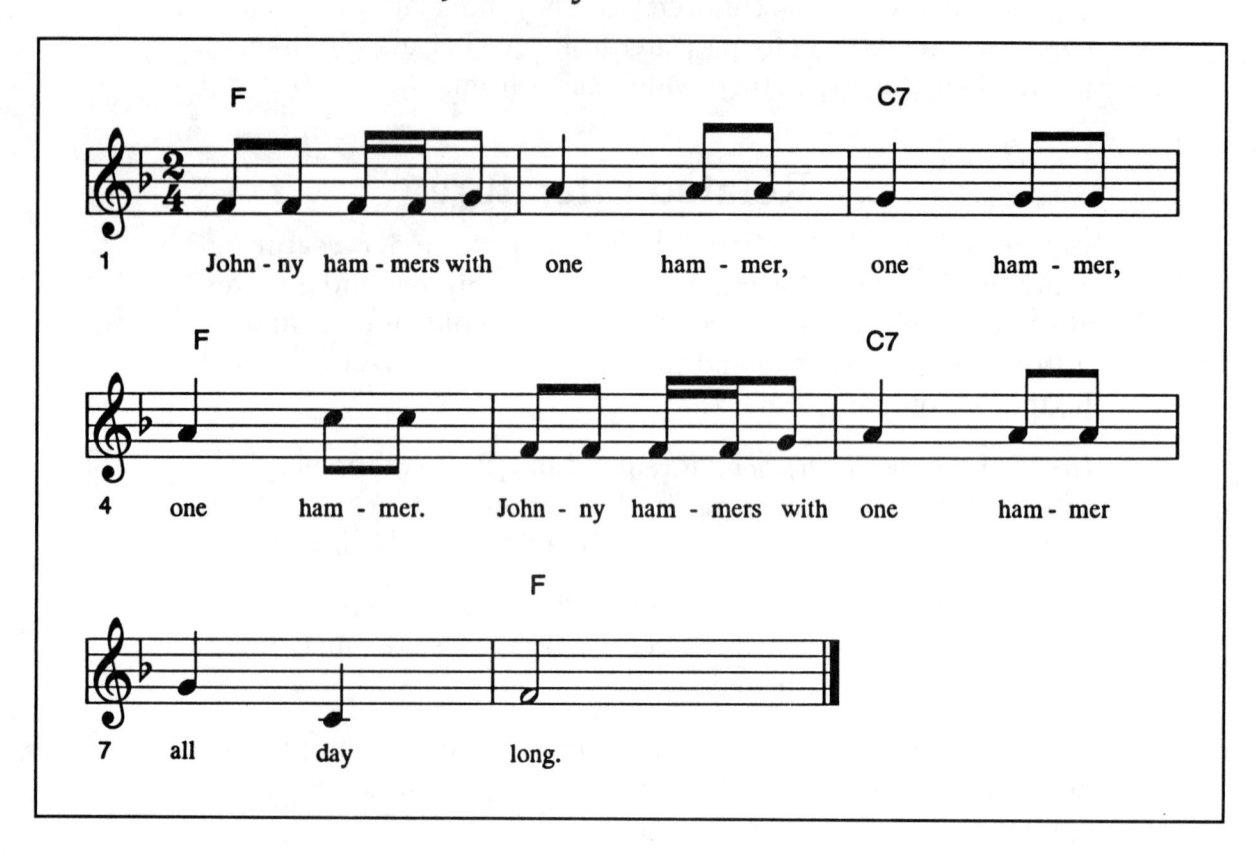

[Sheet music in 2/4 time, key of F]

1. John-ny ham-mers with one ham-mer, one ham-mer,
4. one ham-mer. John-ny ham-mers with one ham-mer
7. all day long.

Additional verses

. . . 2 hammers . . .

. . . 3 hammers . . .

. . . 4 hammers . . .

. . . 5 hammers . . .

Music Expansion

Point to one of the children as the song is sung. Use that child's name in the song. Then have that child point to another child whose name will be used in the next verse. Continue until all children have had a turn. (Increase the number of hammers with each child.)

Invite children to use rhythm sticks or other instruments to keep the beat. Start off with one child or group playing one type of instrument. Add another child or group with a different instrument each time the song increases a number.

Vary the loudness and softness of the "hammering." Model for children using drums, rhythm sticks, or clapping to demonstrate how the same object can sound loud or soft. Then sing the song again and indicate how children should play instruments or clap. Stress the words *loud, louder, loudest, soft, softer,* and *softest*.

Themes

Community Helpers
Construction
Counting/Numbers

Featured Book

Building a House by Byron Barton

Curriculum Integration

Choose activities from the following curriculum areas that fit your teaching style and the needs and interests of the children.

Science

Invite several children to pound on various surfaces such as a table, a chair, a wall, their chests, or a pillow. Encourage children to talk about the sounds using forms of the words *loud* and *soft*.

Read *Building a House*. Point out some of the tools in the book and then show children the actual tools. Provide an area for a workbench and tools. Place safety glasses, hard hats, scrap lumber, levels, rulers, hammers, screwdrivers, wrenches, nails, screws, nuts, and bolts in the area. (Lumberyards are good sources for scrap lumber. Be sure to use soft wood such as redwood, cedar, or pine.) Demonstrate how to use the tools or invite a professional in to talk to the children. Ask children to make a class list of safety rules to post in the area. An alternative activity is to invite children to hammer golf tees into Styrofoam blocks.

Math

Provide nuts, bolts, screws, and nails. Invite children to sort the items and discuss how they sorted the items.

Offer children a variety of sizes of nuts, washers, and bolts. Have children match nuts and washers to bolts and screw them together.

Art

Encourage children to pound on clay with their fists or open hands. After they have spent time manipulating the clay with their fists and hands, ask children what tools they could use to make something with the clay. Explain that a tool is any item that helps get a job done. For example, a craft stick could be a tool for clay. Then provide several of the tools children suggested.

Invite children to make tool-collage paintings. Have them dip plastic or old tools into paint and then press the tools on sheets of paper. Offer several colors of paint for the children's use. Display the tool collages on a bulletin board or wall.

Reading/Writing

Read *Building a House*. As you read the book a second time, have children name the workers in the book. Ask children how they think the workers help each other to finish the house.

Sing "Johnny Hammers" again. Ask children what they think Johnny is hammering. Invite children to brainstorm a list of other things that can be built. Write their responses on chart paper. Invite children to draw pictures of the items on the list. Then post each picture beside the item it depicts. Encourage children to add to the list.

Ask children what they would build if they had a hammer. Who would use it? How would it be used? Suggest they draw pictures of what they would build. Then have children write or dictate something about their pictures. Bind the children's pictures together to make a book titled *If I Had a Hammer*. Teach them the song by the same name.

Social Studies

Ask a construction worker to come to the class and talk about building, tools, and safety rules. Encourage children to ask questions.

Arrange to visit a construction site. Talk with workers about their jobs. If possible, visit the same site several times and have children observe the changes that take place.

Related Literature

Building a House by Byron Barton. Through brilliantly simple words and pictures the reader follows each step, and soon a house is built. Morrow, 1981.

The Little House by Virginia Lee Burton. A cleverly illustrated story of a little house that becomes a victim of the accelerating tempo of city life. Houghton Mifflin, 1978.

Martin's Hats by Joan W. Blos. A variety of hats afford Martin many adventures. Morrow, 1984.

Mike Mulligan and His Steam Shovel by Virginia Lee Burton. By remaining faithful to his steam shovel against the threat of the new gas- and diesel-engine contraptions, Mike Mulligan digs his way to a surprising and happy ending. Houghton Mifflin, 1939.

Whose Hat Is That? by Ron Roy. Photos show the different kinds of hats people wear. Houghton Mifflin, 1987.

Kumbaya

Additional verse

Someone's singing . . .

(Change the word *Lord* to *friends* if desired.)

Music Expansion

Explain that this is an African-American song. The words roughly mean *come by here*.

Substitute one of the children's names for the word *someone*.

Invite children to make up new verses for the song and act them out. Record their ideas on chart paper. They might suggest ideas such as someone's eating, someone's walking, or someone's sneezing.

Themes

Animals
Cultures
Emotions/Feelings

Featured Book

Ashanti to Zulu: African Traditions by Margaret Musgrove

Curriculum Integration

Choose activities from the following curriculum areas that fit your teaching style and the needs and interests of the children.

Science

Display plastic replicas of animals native to Africa. Help children identify the animals. Some of the animals are listed below.

rhinoceroses	giraffes	elephants
lions	gazelles	zebras
gorillas	monkeys	crocodiles
hippopotamuses	ostriches	flamingos
snakes	antelope	buffalo
cheetahs	hyenas	jackals
leopards	chimpanzees	pelicans
storks		

Invite children to taste foods that are grown on African farms. These include bananas, oranges, cabbages, cucumbers, tamarinds, star apples, plantains, and cassavas.

Math

Suggest children use the African animals used in Science and count, sort, or classify them.

Invite children to count from one to five or from one to ten. Then help them learn to count in Swahili. Explain that this is a language spoken by people in the eastern countries of Africa.

one	moja	(MO-jah)
two	mbili	(m-BEE-lee)
three	tatu	(TA-too)
four	nne	(N-nay)
five	tano	(TAH-no)
six	sita	(SEE-tah)
seven	saba	(SAH-bah)
eight	nane	(NAH-nay)
nine	tisa	(TEE-sah)
ten	kumi	(KOO-mee)

Art

Show children some actual African wood carvings or pictures of carvings. Invite children to use clay to create their own sculptures. Offer children forks, orange sticks, or toothpicks to scratch designs into their sculptures.

Read *Ashanti to Zulu: African Traditions*. Point out the ceremonial masks that are worn on the pages for the letters D and U. Then invite children to create African masks. Have them spread petroleum jelly over old plastic Halloween masks. Then invite children to mold papier-mâché over the masks. When the masks are dry, help children carefully lift the papier-mâché masks off the Halloween masks. Provide paints, brushes, feathers, beads, construction paper scraps, and glue for children to decorate the masks.

Reading/Writing

Read *Ashanti to Zulu: African Traditions*. Explain that a *tradition* is something that is done by a group of people again and again, year after year. For example, a family might always have a family reunion every year on the third Sunday of July. Invite children to draw pictures of what they think are traditions in their families. When the pictures are completed, have children write or dictate something about the tradition.

Remind children of the new verses they created. (See Music Expansion.) Then ask children what makes them laugh, what makes them cry, and what makes them sing. Invite children to write or dictate stories about one of the feelings. Encourage them to make up titles for their stories such as "Someone's Crying" or "Someone's Laughing."

Social Studies

Invite someone whose first language is native to one of the African countries to visit the class. (Local community groups, high schools, and colleges or universities are good resources.) Invite the guest to talk about traditions in his or her country and the similarities and differences between that country and this one. Suggest that the speaker teach children a few words of the African language.

Arrange a field trip to a museum, art gallery, or store that has a display of African art or other items that reflect the culture.

Related Literature

African Dream by Eloise Greenfield. In her dreams about Africa, a black child sees animals, shops in a marketplace, reads strange words from an old book, and returns to the village where her long-ago granddaddy welcomes her. HarperCollins, 1977.

Ashanti to Zulu: African Traditions by Margaret Musgrove. This alphabet book describes the customs of African tribes. Dial, 1976.

jambo means hello: Swahili Alphabet Book by Muriel Feelings. Illustrated Swahili words from A to Z re-create the traditions of East Africa. Dial, 1975.

moja means one: Swahili Counting Book by Muriel Feelings. A counting book that is a tribute to the heritage of East Africa. Dial, 1971.

Somewhere in Africa by Ingrid Mennen and Niki Daly. A young boy, living in a busy African city, dreams of the wild animals he sees only in books. Dutton, 1990.

Little Bunny Foo Foo

1. Little Bunny Foo Foo, hopping through the
4. forest, scooping up the field mice and
7. bopping 'em on the head.

[SPOKEN] Down came the good fairy, and she said:

9. Little Bunny Foo Foo, I don't want to
12. see you scooping up the field mice and

Little Bunny Foo Foo (continued)

15 bop - ping 'em on the head.

[SPOKEN] I'll give you three chances, and if you don't behave, I'll turn you into a goon! **The next day:** REPEAT SONG

Additional verses

Verse 2 is the same as verse 1 except the spoken part at the end.
I'll give you two more chances . . .

Verse 3 is the same as verse 1 except the spoken part at the end.
I'll give you one more chance . . .

Verse 4 is the same as verse 1 except the spoken part at the end.
I gave you three chances and you didn't behave . . . POOF! You're a goon. The moral of the story is . . . Hare today, goon tomorrow.

Music Expansion

Invite children to change the animals that are scooped up and the habitats where Little Bunny Foo Foo would find the animals. Record children's ideas and post them in the science area. For example, children might include starfish swimming in the ocean or lizards walking through the desert. Then have children sing new verses for the song.

Little Bunny Foo Foo
Swimming in the ocean,
Scooping up the starfish . . .

Encourage children to act out the song. One child could be the bunny, one the good fairy, and the rest of the children could be field mice.

Invite children to play a circle game similar to Duck, Duck, Goose. Have children sit in a circle on the floor. Choose one child to be Bunny Foo Foo and hop around the outside of the circle. That child then chooses a child to be a field mouse and lightly bops (taps) the chosen child on the shoulder. The child who is tapped chases Bunny Foo Foo around the circle until Bunny Foo Foo arrives at the mouse's place and sits down. The mouse then becomes Bunny Foo Foo and continues the game.

Themes

Animals
Habitats

Featured Book

Foolish Rabbit's Big Mistake by Rafe Martin

Curriculum Integration

Choose activities from the following curriculum areas that fit your teaching style and the needs and interests of the children.

Science

Read the list of animals and habitats children created in Music Expansion. Arrange children in small groups and have them select animals and create shoe box habitats for them. Provide shoe boxes, plastic animals, craft sticks, clay, sand, dirt, grass, twigs, a tub of water, or any other materials children might need for the habitats. Some children might make farms, forests, zoos, or oceans in their shoe boxes.

Place sand, dirt, or water in the sand/water table or a large tub. Add plastic animals, shovels, spoons, flour or sugar scoops, and ice cream scoops. Invite children to scoop up the animals with the various "scooping" tools.

Math

Invite children to bring in toy bunnies from home. Have children sort, seriate, measure, weigh, and compare the bunnies. Encourage them to talk about similarities and differences.

Make a chart with three columns with pictorial headings for land, sky, and water. Hang it on a wall at the children's level. Then invite children to cut pictures from magazines of animals and decide in which of the three places the animals would be found most often. Have children glue the animals in the appropriate columns. When children are finished, talk about which column has *more* and which has *fewer*.

Art

Read *Foolish Rabbit's Big Mistake*. Point out that the illustrations are done in pastels, or chalk. Provide children with colored paper and chalk and invite them to create a picture. Demonstrate how to blend the colors by gently rubbing with a finger or a tissue. To reduce smudging, spray the completed pictures with a commercial spray or hair spray.

Provide a variety of art materials such as clay, construction paper, markers, chalk, paints, and paper. Ask children to create the goon that Little Bunny Foo Foo was changed into.

Reading/Writing

Read *Foolish Rabbit's Big Mistake*. Then sing the song again. Ask children how the song and the story are alike. What mistakes did Foolish Rabbit and Little Bunny Foo Foo make? What might each have done to keep from making the mistake? Ask children to talk about mistakes they or people they know may have made. Discuss what they might have done to avoid the mistake.

Invite children to write or dictate stories about what happened to Foolish Rabbit or Little Bunny Foo Foo the next day.

Social Studies

Discuss with children why they think Little Bunny Foo Foo was bopping the mice on the head. Invite children to talk about other ways Little Bunny Foo Foo might have treated the mice. Then encourage children to role-play situations on resolving conflicts or dealing with someone who is treating them unkindly.

Take children to a park or nature preserve and have them observe animals in their natural surroundings.

Related Literature

Chicken Little by Steven Kellogg. Chicken Little and her feathered friends are all a-flutter when she gets a mysterious bump on the head. Morrow, 1985.

Foolish Rabbit's Big Mistake by Rafe Martin. As all the animals panic and flee at little rabbit's announcement that the earth is breaking up, a brave lion steps in and brings sense to the situation. Sandcastle, 1985.

Henny Penny by Paul Galdone. Bold pictures and a subtle twist at the end distinguish this new version of the familiar folktale. Clarion, 1979.

The Runaway Bunny by Margaret Wise Brown. This is a comforting story of a bunny's imaginary game of hide-and-seek and the loving mother who finds him every time. HarperCollins, 1942.

Who Lives Here? by Dot and Sy Barlowe. Seven environments from pond to prairie—and more than 100 animals that inhabit them—are described in clear text and large, realistic pictures. Random, 1980.

London Bridge

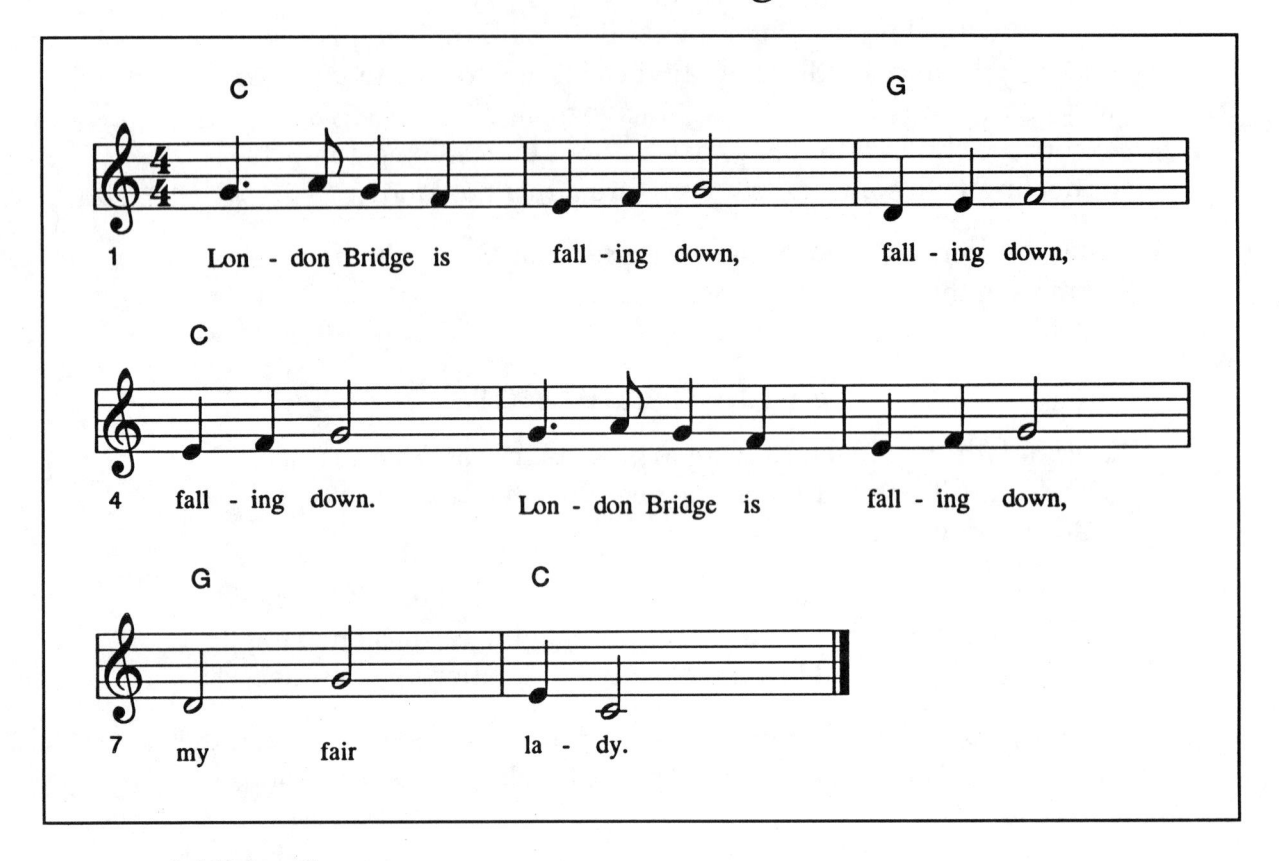

1 Lon - don Bridge is fall - ing down, fall - ing down,
4 fall - ing down. Lon - don Bridge is fall - ing down,
7 my fair la - dy.

Additional verse

Take the keys and lock her up,
Lock her up, lock her up.
Take the keys and lock her up,
My fair lady.

Music Expansion

Invite two children to form a bridge by facing each other and holding each other's hands in the air. Have the other children stand in a line and walk under the bridge. On the words *my fair lady*, the two children drop their hands to capture the child walking under. As the second verse is sung, the captured child is rocked between the arms of the two children. The captured child then chooses someone to be the bridge with him or her, and the song is sung again.

Instead of singing *my fair lady*, suggest children sing the captured child's name—*my fair Lindsey*. Or change *lady* to *laddie* if a boy is captured.

Make an obstacle course in the classroom or on the playground. Designate one area of the obstacle course where children will get caught when *my fair lady* is sung. Invite the child who is "captured" in that area when the first verse ends to think of an action for everyone to copy as they sing a second verse:

> Show us something we can do,
> We can do, we can do.
> Show us something we can do,
> And we'll do it too.

Themes

Construction
Folklore and Tales
Nursery Rhymes
Position Words

Featured Book

The Three Billy Goats Gruff retold by Paul Galdone

Curriculum Integration

Choose activities from the following curriculum areas that fit your teaching style and the needs and interests of the children.

Social Studies

Explain that *bridges* are structures that help people get from one side of an obstacle to another by crossing over the obstacle. Bridges don't always go over water. There are bridges in malls that go across a lower level. There are pedestrian bridges so people can safely cross busy streets. And there are even runway bridges over roads for airplanes. Take children to different places in the area where there are bridges. Help children notice what the bridge is spanning.

Science

Show pictures of the London Bridge and explain how it was taken apart and moved from London, England, to Lake Havasu, Arizona. In the block area, invite children to construct a bridge or another structure and then experiment with ways to move it and reconstruct it.

Show children pictures of bridges. Pictures should show bridges that span bodies of water, roads, or other obstacles. Then ask children to brainstorm ways they could cross each obstacle if there were no bridge. Record the responses on chart paper and post with each picture.

Math

Place locks and keys in a math discovery area. Invite children to sort them by type, number, color, or size. Then encourage children to find the correct key to unlock each lock.

Read *The Three Billy Goats Gruff*. Then invite children to talk about small, medium, and big sizes. Provide groups of the same item in three different sizes and have children sort and then arrange them by size. Items might include forks, spoons, cups, bowls, buttons, or cutout shapes.

Art

Invite children to construct bridges. Provide materials such as craft sticks, twigs, ropes, blocks, clay, glue, paper, pipe cleaners, or other items. Display the finished bridges on a table in the art area.

Provide children with paper bags, markers, crayons, collage materials, construction paper scraps, paper tubes, yarn, and glue. Invite them to make troll masks. Help children cut holes for eyes in the bags and then have them decorate the masks.

Reading/Writing

Read *The Three Billy Goats Gruff*. Then ask children to tell other ways the goats might have convinced the troll to let them cross the bridge. Could they have found a way to make friends with the troll? What do they think happened to the troll to make him so mean? Could the goats have done something to make him kinder?

Invite children to write a group story about what might happen when the goats try to cross the bridge again or if someone else meets the troll. Have children take turns creating sentences or phrases. Write their responses on a large sheet of chart paper. Encourage children to continue until they decide the story is finished. (Read the story at intervals to remind children what has already been dictated.) Then read the final story to them. Suggest children illustrate parts of the story. Hang the story and illustrations on a bulletin board or wall.

Make a flannel board of the story. Encourage children to retell the story using position words such as *over, around, under, beside,* and *on*.

Related Literature

London Bridge Is Falling Down by Peter Spier. A favorite childhood song is beautifully illustrated in picture-book form. Doubleday, 1972.

over, under & through by Tana Hoban. Photographs demonstrate the spatial concepts expressed in twelve words such as *around, between, against,* and *behind*. Atheneum, 1973.

The Three Billy Goats Gruff retold by Paul Galdone. The book retells a folktale about three Billy Goats who get even with a menacing troll. Clarion, 1973.

Mary's Wearing a Red Dress

1 Ma-ry's wearing a red dress, a red dress, a
4 red dress. Ma-ry's wearing a red dress
7 all day long.

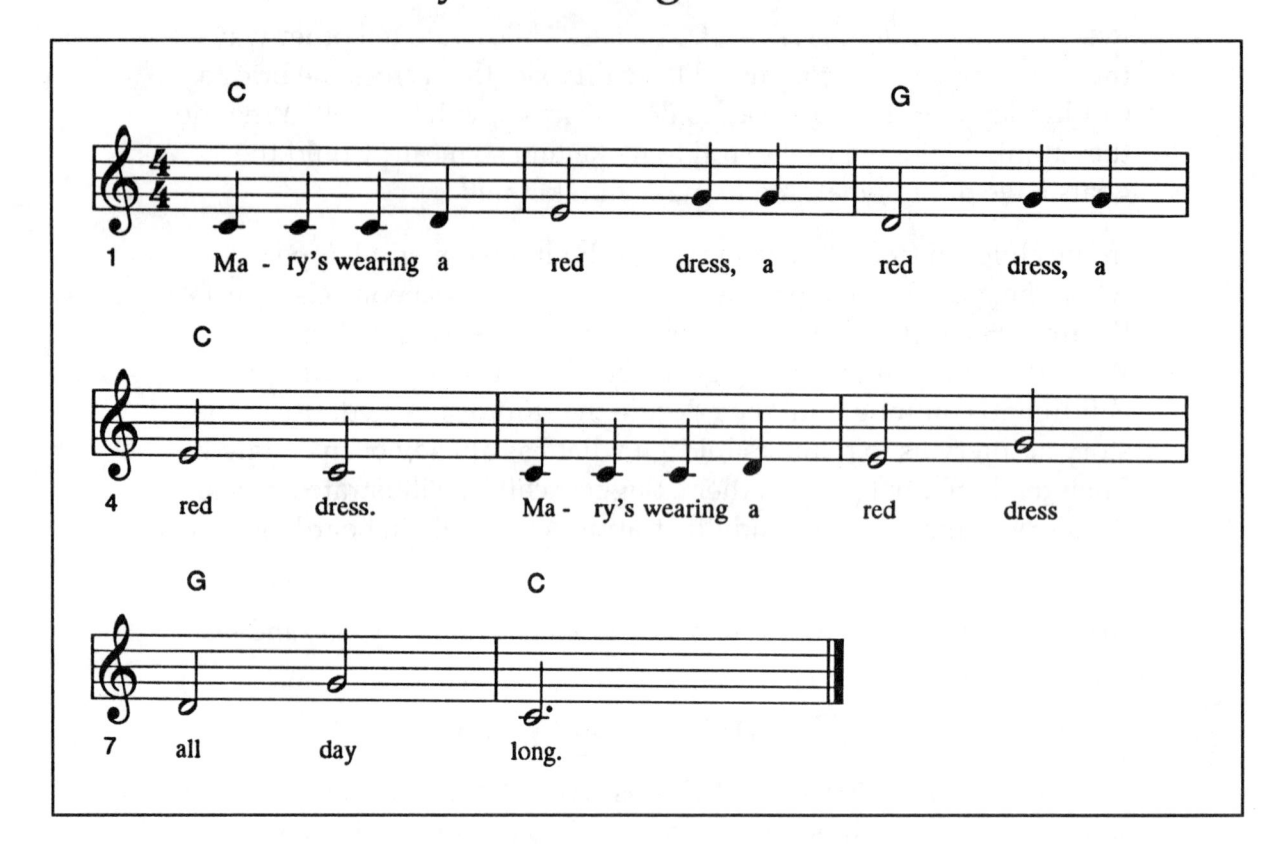

Music Expansion

Sing about something each child is wearing without using his or her name and invite children to guess who the child is.

> Someone's wearing a purple shirt,
> A purple shirt, a purple shirt.
> Someone's wearing a purple shirt.
> Who can it be?

Invite children to choose an emotion or feeling and show the emotion with their faces or body actions. Then sing about the feeling or emotion.

> Josh is wearing a sad face,
> A sad face, a sad face.
> Josh is wearing a sad face.
> Whose turn is next?

Themes

Clothing
Colors
Emotions/Feelings
Self-Awareness

Featured Book

Quick as a Cricket by Audrey Wood

Curriculum Integration

Choose activities from the following curriculum areas that fit your teaching style and the needs and interests of the children.

Science

Invite children to make colors. Explain that most colors are made from combinations of red, yellow, and blue. Provide food coloring, water in clear cups or glasses, eyedroppers, and stirring sticks. Have children place one drop of food coloring at a time into the water. Encourage them to gently stir the colored water after each addition and talk about the changes that occur. Have children place clean water in the cups or glasses before trying other combinations.

Place color paddles in the science area. Suggest children look around the room through the paddles and talk about how things look. Encourage children to place one paddle over the other and observe the color changes.

Art

Place different colors of construction paper in the art area. Invite children to make color collages. Have them cut pictures from old catalogs or magazines. Then have children decide which colors are represented by the pictures and glue them on the appropriate colors of construction paper.

Read *Quick as a Cricket*. Discuss the different feelings that are shown in the book. Talk about the colors that the illustrator used to convey the feelings. For example, display the pages showing *sad* and *happy*. Ask children if there are colors that make them feel differently. Then invite children to draw pictures of themselves showing a feeling. Children may want to use colors that help convey the feeling they've chosen to show. Suggest they share their pictures with the class and have others guess what feeling is shown in each picture.

Math

Make a graph of colors. Across the bottom of a sheet of graph paper, write the color names using a marker or crayon of the same color. (Print the word *white* with a black marker. Or write the word in white on a small piece of black or dark blue paper and glue it to the chart.) Then have children write their names or initials in the spaces above all the colors that they are wearing. Talk about the graph. Is there a color that everyone is wearing? Is there a color that no one is wearing? Which color is being worn by the most children? the fewest?

Social Studies

Bring in or show pictures of clothing traditional to other cultures such as a beret from France, a serape from Mexico, and a kimono from Japan. Have children talk about similarities and differences between their clothing and clothing from other cultures. (To avoid stereotyping, mention that not all people from that culture wear these items daily.)

Choose one day a week to have a color day. Have the class vote on what special color they would like to have for each day. Encourage children to wear articles of clothing in the color. Make available in the art area paints, crayons, markers, and paper of that color. Invite children to help make a snack that reflects the color of the day. For example, for red the children might choose apples, strawberries, or cherry gelatin.

Invite children to play a game called Police Officer, Please Find My Lost Child. Have the group sit on the floor and then choose one child to be the police officer. Ask the police officer to stand in the middle of the circle and find the lost child. Describe one of the other children. Have the police officer search for the lost child by using the description given. When the police officer has located the child, have him or her identify that child. That child then becomes the next police officer.

Reading/Writing

Read *Quick as a Cricket*. Talk about the animals that are associated with the feelings shown in the book. Ask children what other animals they could associate with the emotions and feelings. Write children's responses on chart paper and invite them to illustrate the phrases.

Make a book about the song using the class as the starring characters. Have a photograph or drawing of each child and invite him or her to decide which item of clothing to write a song verse about. Glue the pictures or drawings on sheets of paper and have children dictate or write the song verse next to the picture. Bind the pages together to make a songbook. Show the book as children sing the new verses.

Related Literature

The Berenstain Kids: I Love Colors by Stan and Jan Berenstain. Two youngsters describe things that are red, yellow, orange, beige, pink, and other colors. Random, 1987.

Hailstones and Halibut Bones by Mary O'Neill. This fascinating book teaches the concept of colors by developing some of the other senses. Doubleday, 1973.

I Like Me! by Nancy Carlson. A simple story about a little pig who feels good about herself and her accomplishments. Penguin, 1990.

Mary Wore Her Red Dress, and Henry Wore His Green Sneakers by Merle Peek. On Kate's birthday all of her animal friends come to the party dressed in clothes of a different color. Houghton Mifflin, 1988.

Quick as a Cricket by Audrey Wood. Large, colorful illustrations celebrate a child's growing self-awareness. Child's Play, 1982.

Miss Polly Had a Dolly

G
D7
1 Miss Pol-ly had a dol -ly who was sick, sick, sick. So she
G
4 called for the doc - tor to come quick, quick, quick. The
D7
6 doc - tor came__ with his bag and his hat. And he
D7
G
8 knocked on the door__ with a rat - tat - tat.

Additional verse
He looked at the dolly, and he shook his head.
And he said, "Miss Polly, put her straight to bed!"
He wrote on the paper for some pills, pills, pills.
"I'll be back in the morning with the bills, bills, bills."

Music Expansion

Change the genders in the song in order to promote the nurturing aspect of boys with dolls and the idea that girls can be doctors.

Use a child's name in the room instead of "Miss Polly," and that child can hold the doll as the group sings.

Invite children to dramatize the song. Provide dolls, doll beds, white shirts or smocks for doctors, doctors' kits, pencils, and paper in the drama area.

This is a good clapping song. Have children just pat their knees or sit facing a partner and clap hands together. Children might enjoy facing another child and doing a clapping pattern such as clap their own hands, clap the partner's hands (repeat); or pat knees, clap hands (repeat).

Suggest that instead of a dolly, Miss Polly might have a puppy or a kitty. Whom would she call? Write new verses with the class.

Themes

Community Helpers
Drug Awareness
Health

Featured Book

The Berenstain Bears Go to the Doctor by Stan and Jan Berenstain

Curriculum Integration

Choose activities from the following curriculum areas that fit your teaching style and the needs and interests of the children.

Science

Provide a real stethoscope and invite children to listen to their own heartbeat and the heartbeats of others.

Make a health care discovery table in the science area. Include items such as stethoscopes, blood pressure cuffs, tongue depressors, eye charts, scales, bandages of various sizes, and surgical masks and caps. Encourage children to handle the items and talk about experiences they have had with doctors and nurses.

Read *The Berenstain Bears Go to the Doctor* and invite children to talk about why people need to visit doctors. Then ask children what they can do to stay healthy. Record children's responses on a chart with the heading "I Stay Healthy by . . . "

Math

Invite children to bring dolls or stuffed animals from home. Suggest children compare size, colors, and other attributes of the dolls and animals.

Give children different numbers of tongue depressors. Have each child count his or her tongue depressors. Make a graph of the numbers. Ask children questions about the graph such as who has the most, the fewest, and the same. Then count the total number of tongue depressors.

Set out different sizes of bandages in the math area. Invite children to sort them by size or place them in size order.

Art

Provide children with cotton balls, bandages, tongue depressors, glue, and paper. Suggest children make a collage with the items.

Explain that doctor is one occupation that children might choose one day. Ask children to draw pictures of themselves in a chosen occupation. Then have them write or dictate something about the pictures.

Reading/Writing

Read *The Berenstain Bears Go to the Doctor*. Have children talk about visits to their own doctors. Ask them to describe the office and the workers.

Display a picture of a doctor or nurse examining someone. Invite children to write a class story about the picture. Display the picture and the story on a wall or bulletin board.

Social Studies

Invite a doctor or nurse to come in and talk with children about staying healthy. Suggest the guest bring in items he or she uses at the office or hospital. Encourage children to ask questions.

Use this song to introduce a discussion of drug awareness. Emphasize that it is only safe for children to take drugs prescribed to them by a doctor and only in the prescribed amount. Talk about the dangers of accepting drugs from anyone other than the doctor or parents. Discuss what to do if anyone ever approaches them with drugs. Arrange with someone from the police department or other agency with a children's drug-awareness program to come in and talk with the children.

Related Literature

The Berenstain Bears and the Drug-Free Zone by Stan and Jan Berenstain. Sister and Brother uncover a drug problem in bear country, and they're determined to track down the culprits. Random, 1993.

The Berenstain Bears Go to the Doctor by Stan and Jan Berenstain. Mama and Papa Bear take the cubs to the doctor for a checkup only to find that Papa Bear is the one who is sick. Random, 1981.

Curious George Goes to the Hospital by Margaret and H. A. Rey. Curious George has an unexpected stay in the hospital. Houghton Mifflin, 1973.

William's Doll by Charlotte Zolotow. William wants a doll more than anything. Then one day someone really understands his wish and makes it easy for others to understand too. HarperCollins, 1972.

The More We Are Together

1 The more we are to-geth-er, to-
4 geth-er, to-geth-er, the more we are to-
7 geth-er the hap-pi-er we'll be. For
10 your friends are my friends, and my friends are
13 your friends. The more we are to-geth-er the
16 hap-pi-er we'll be.

Additional verse

The more we share together, together, together . . .
For sharing is caring, and caring is sharing . . .

Music Expansion

Invite children to brainstorm things that friends do together. Write their responses on the chalkboard or on chart paper. Then have children make up new verses to sing.

Have children use instruments and sing. Suggest they freeze, or stop all action, when they sing the word *stop*. For example:

We're playing all together, together, together,
We're playing all together, and now we will stop.

Or use a child's name and instrument and end the song with *and who will be next?* For example:

Todd is playing bells, the bells, the bells,
Todd is playing bells, and who will be next?

Or isolate the various instruments. For example:

We're playing just the rhythm sticks, the rhythm sticks, the rhythm sticks;
We're playing just the rhythm sticks, and now we will stop.

Ask children to think of movements to be used in the song. Then invite them to use their suggestions as they sing. For example:

We're jumping in the classroom . . .

Themes

Family
Friends
Shapes
Time

Featured Book

May I Bring a Friend? by Beatrice Schenk de Regniers

Curriculum Integration

Choose activities from the following curriculum areas that fit your teaching style and the needs and interests of the children.

Science

Place magnets and various small objects in the science area. Encourage children to experiment with the magnets. Which items come together with the magnets? Which items don't?

Math

Use tape to make shape outlines on the floor such as triangles, squares, or circles. Have one child at a time step into the shape. Then invite children to count the number of children that came together in each shape.

Purchase or make Things That Go Together cards. Encourage children to match the things that go together. Some items they might match include a hammer and a nail, a dog and a leash, and a fish and a fishbowl.

Read *May I Bring a Friend?* Then show children a calendar. Invite them to say the days of the week. Introduce the concepts of *today*, *tomorrow*, and *yesterday*. Say "Today the boy brings a hippopotamus." Ask the children to look in the book and find what the boy brought yesterday and what he will bring tomorrow.

Art

Invite children to make a collage of people getting together. Have them cut pictures from magazines showing people doing things together. Suggest they glue the pictures on large mural paper and talk about the pictures they chose.

Have children think about what they like to do when they get together with family or friends. Then provide a choice of art media and invite children to create pictures showing what they like to do with family or friends. Suggest children write or dictate something about their pictures.

Reading/Writing

Read *May I Bring a Friend?* Ask children what they think the boy does on days he doesn't get together with the king and queen. Does he have other friends? If so, what might the boy do with the other friends?

Provide each child with a 1" x 6" strip of construction paper. Ask each child to write or dictate something that he or she likes to do with the class. Then have children link their strips together to form a paper friendship chain.

Social Studies

Remind children that the king and queen first invited the boy to join them for tea. Help children plan a "tea" for parents, grandparents, or another class. Encourage children to plan the refreshments, the activities, and the invitations for their get-together.

Invite a class of older children to act as "big brothers and big sisters" to the class. Suggest they get together for a fun activity. The get-together could begin with the song. Then the older children could play games with the younger children, help them with an art project, or read to them. This could become a monthly event.

Related Literature

Can You Match This? by Rick and Ann Walton. Jokes are made about unlikely pairs of things. First Avenue, 1989.

Do You Want to Be My Friend? by Eric Carle. A little mouse wants someone to play with. But he has to follow a lot of tails before he can find just the right companion. HarperCollins, 1987.

I Go with My Family to Grandma's by Riki Levinson. Dozens of cousins and their families, from all corners of New York City, converge on Grandma's house for a fun-filled reunion. Dutton, 1986.

May I Bring a Friend? by Beatrice Schenk de Regniers. A little boy is invited to tea by the king and queen and brings along some unusual friends. Aladdin, 1974.

Some Things Go Together by Charlotte Zolotow. Illustrations accompany couplets describing things that go together naturally such as "sand with sea" and especially "you and me." HarperCollins, 1987.

The Muffin Man

[Musical notation with lyrics:]

Oh, do you know the muf-fin man, the muf-fin man, the muf-fin man? Oh, do you know the muf-fin man who lives on Dru-ry Lane?

Additional verse

Oh, yes, I know the muffin man,
The muffin man, the muffin man.
Oh, yes, I know the muffin man
Who lives on Drury Lane.

Music Expansion

Sing about various community helpers and where they work.

> Do you know the bus driver . . .
> Who drives our school bus?

Use this song to help children learn their addresses. Substitute the child's name for *the muffin man* and the child's address for *Drury Lane*. (Either squeeze in syllables as you sing or speak the address.)

Themes

Community Helpers
Food/Nutrition
Health

Featured Book

Martin's Hats by Joan W. Blos

Curriculum Integration

Choose activities from the following curriculum areas that fit your teaching style and the needs and interests of the children.

Math

Make a graph of children's favorite kinds of muffins.

Provide a variety of sorting items such as buttons, beads, and color chips. Invite children to sort the items into muffin tins.

Read *Martin's Hats*. Talk about the different hats people wear when they work. Invite children to play a matching game. Provide them with pictures of people at work and pictures of hats people wear at work. Encourage children to match the hats to the workers. Some of the pictures might include a baseball player and a cap, a baker and a baker's hat, a construction worker and a hard hat, and a fire fighter and a fire fighter's helmet.

Science

Invite children to make muffins for a snack using the recipe on the next page.

Fruity Muffins

Ingredients

1 3/4 cups flour
1/4 cup sugar
2 1/2 teaspoons baking powder
3/4 teaspoon salt
1 egg
3/4 cup milk
1/3 cup cooking oil
1/2 cup finely chopped fruit
　(apple, banana, or cherry)

Utensils

cupcake papers
muffin pan
measuring cups
measuring spoons
medium mixing bowl
mixing spoon
small mixing bowl
fork

Place cupcake papers in the muffin pan. Measure dry ingredients into the medium mixing bowl. Stir to combine. Use a fork to beat together the egg, milk, and oil in the small bowl. Pour the egg mixture over the flour mixture. Stir until dry ingredients are moistened. There will be lumps. Fold in chopped fruit. Fill muffin cups 3/4 full of batter. Bake for 20-25 minutes in a 400°F oven. Makes 12 muffins.

Encourage children to wash their hands and gather the ingredients and utensils needed. Suggest they measure the ingredients and observe any changes that take place as the ingredients are combined and the muffins are baked.

　Later, remind children that they ate the muffins for a snack. Ask them what else they would have with the muffins to make a nutritious breakfast. What would they include with the muffins for lunch? for dinner? Record children's responses on three separate sheets of chart paper.

Art

Talk about nutritious foods and "junk" foods. Then invite children to make collages showing nutritious foods and junk foods. Provide two large sheets of mural paper—one with the heading "Nutritious Food" and the other with the heading "Junk Food." Ask children to cut food pictures from magazines. Have them decide if the food is nutritious or not and glue the pictures to the appropriate sheet of mural paper.

Reading/Writing

Read *Martin's Hats*. Ask children what other adventures Martin might have if he were to wear other hats. Invite children to write a group story about another adventure Martin could have. Provide a variety of hats or pictures of hats to use as cues for children.

Invite children to publish a class cookbook. Have each child think of a food that he or she likes. Encourage children to dictate or write the recipes on recipe-card shaped paper. Then suggest children draw pictures of the food after it's been prepared. Bind the recipes and illustrations together to make the cookbook. Have the book available for children to take home and share.

Social Studies

Arrange a visit to a bakery. Ask a worker to talk about the job and any special clothing or equipment the job requires. Or ask a professional baker to come into your classroom and prepare a special project with children.

Related Literature

The Little Red Hen retold by Paul Galdone. This favorite tale tells of an industrious little hen and a lazy cat, dog, and mouse. Houghton Mifflin, 1979.

Martin's Hats by Joan W. Blos. A variety of hats affords Martin many adventures. Morrow, 1984.

The Train by David McPhail. Late one night Matthew boards his toy train and embarks on a fantastic journey of the imagination. Little, 1977.

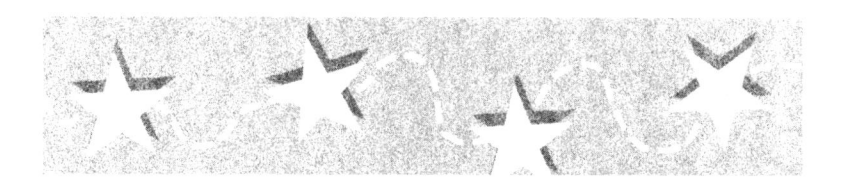

What's It Like to Be a . . . Series. This informative series tells about the work involved in a variety of professions.

What's It Like to Be a . . . Bus Driver by Judith Stamper. Troll, 1990.

What's It Like to Be a . . . Chef by Susan C. Poskanzer. Troll, 1990.

What's It Like to Be a . . . Dentist by Judith Stamper. Troll, 1989.

What's It Like to Be a . . . Doctor by Judith Bauer. Troll, 1990.

What's It Like to Be a . . . Farmer by Morgan Matthews. Troll, 1990.

What's It Like to Be a . . . Grocer by Shelley Wilks. Troll, 1990.

What's It Like to Be a . . . Newspaper Reporter by Janet Craig. Troll, 1989.

What's It Like to Be a . . . Nurse by Judith Bauer. Troll, 1990.

What's It Like to Be a . . . Police Officer by Michael J. Pellowski. Troll, 1990.

What's It Like to Be a . . . Postal Worker by Morgan Matthews. Troll, 1990.

What's It Like to Be a . . . Railroad Worker by Morgan Matthews. Troll, 1989.

What's It Like to Be a . . . Veterinarian by Judith Stamper. Troll, 1990.

What's It Like to Be an . . . Airline Pilot by Judith Bauer. Troll, 1990.

What's It Like to Be an . . . Astronaut by Judith Bauer. Troll, 1990.

Old MacDonald

1 Old Mac-Don-ald had a farm, E-I-E-I-
4 O. And on his farm he had some chicks,
7 E-I-E-I-O. With a chick, chick here and a
10 chick, chick there. Here a chick, there a chick, ev'rywhere a chick, chick.
13 Old Mac-Don-ald had a farm, E-I-E-I-
16 O.

Additional verse

Old MacDonald had a cow . . .

Music Expansion

Ask children what else they think Old MacDonald could have besides a farm. Some suggestions might include a circus, a forest, a zoo, or a house. Have children decide what would belong there and what type of sounds would be appropriate. Write the responses on the chalkboard or on chart paper as children brainstorm. Point out that the sounds don't always have to come from animals.

Sing "Mixed-up MacDonald Had a Farm." Invite children to pick an animal and give it the wrong sound. For example, a pig says "moo." (Sing the new verses without adding on previous animal sounds.)

Invite children to use instruments and sing "Old MacDonald Had a Band." As they sing about each instrument, the child or group of children with that particular instrument can play.

Themes

Animals
Farms
Growing Things

Featured Book

Barn Dance! by Bill Martin Jr. and John Archambault

Curriculum Integration

Choose activities from the following curriculum areas that fit your teaching style and the needs and interests of the children.

Science

Ask children what crops they think Old MacDonald might grow on his farm. Then show seeds for farm crops such as corn, wheat, fruit, or another crop grown in your area. Display pictures of things the crops are used for. Encourage children, with the help of parents, to look for things at home that come from farm crops. Have them bring in samples, empty boxes, or containers of the products. Display the items on a table in the science area.

Math

Place plastic farm animals in the math area. Encourage children to sort the animals. They might choose to sort the animals by color, number of legs, or type. Encourage them to talk about which group has more, fewer, or the same number of animals.

Provide farm animals for the flannel board. Invite children to count animals as they place them on the flannel board. Have children take one away and then count how many are left.

Art

Invite children to create animals for a mixed-up MacDonald's farm. Suggest children make their mixed-up animals by cutting different animal body parts from magazines and gluing them together on construction paper. For example, a child may choose a combination of a horse's body, a chicken's head, and a pig's tail. Some children may choose to do drawings of their mixed-up animals. Place the animals on an Old MacDonald Mixed-Up-Animal Bulletin Board.

Place paper lunch bags, old socks, scraps of felt, ribbon, buttons, and yarn in the art center. Encourage children to make animal puppets to use as they sing the song.

Read *Barn Dance!* aloud to children. Talk with them about scarecrows. Why do they think farmers use scarecrows? Help children notice what the scarecrow is made of. Do they think he is real? Why or why not? Then arrange children in small groups and invite them to make scarecrows. Provide paper bags, newspapers, markers or crayons, old jeans or overalls, shirts, and old hats. Have children fill paper bags with crumpled newspapers and tie the opening shut to make heads. Then suggest they use the markers or crayons to create facial details. Have children lay the jeans or overalls and shirts on the floor and stuff them with newspapers to make the bodies. Help children set the bodies in corners of the room and then place the heads on top of the bodies. Suggest children add old hats to finish the scarecrows. When they are finished, encourage children to name the scarecrows and place name cards next to them.

Reading/Writing

Invite children to make an Old MacDonald Farm book. Cut out barn-shaped pages and give each child one. Have each child search through magazines for a picture of a favorite animal, cut it out, and glue it onto the page. Some children may prefer to draw their favorite animals. Then suggest children dictate or write stories about their animals or why those animals are their favorites.

Read *Barn Dance!* Then encourage children to think of their pets or pets they would like to have. Ask children to think about what the pets might do at night after everyone is asleep. Invite children to write a group story or individual stories about such happenings. Invite children who chose to write individual stories to share them with the rest of the class. Display the stories in a prominent place in the room.

Social Studies

Arrange a visit to a farm or a petting zoo that features farm animals. Help children identify the animals.

Remind children that in *Barn Dance!* the animals were square dancing. Ask the music teacher or a member of a local square dance club to come in and teach children some simple square dance steps.

Related Literature

Barn Dance! by Bill Martin Jr. and John Archambault. Unable to sleep on the night of a full moon, a young boy follows the sound of music across the fields and finds an unusual barn dance in progress. Holt, 1986.

Early Morning in the Barn by Nancy Tafuri. The youngest readers will laugh and learn as they identify each barnyard animal with its own special sound in this boldly illustrated book. Penguin, 1986.

Farm Alphabet Book by Jane Miller. Outstanding photos of life on a farm make this an exceptionally striking and handsome introduction to the farm and the ABCs. Scholastic, 1982.

Old Farm, New Farm by Felicia Law. This picture book shows the variety of animals, crops, machinery, and buildings on farms. Stevens, 1986.

Once upon MacDonald's Farm by Stephen Gammell. This beautifully illustrated book offers a whimsical, fun-filled version of the song "Old MacDonald." Aladdin, 1990.

Pawpaw Patch

(Sheet music in 4/4, key of F, with chords F, C, F, C, F)

Lyrics under music:
1. Where, oh where is dear lit-tle John-ny? Where, oh where is
4. dear lit-tle John-ny? Where, oh where is dear lit-tle John-ny?
7. Way down yon-der in the paw-paw patch.

Additional verse

Picking up pawpaws and put them in your pocket,
Picking up pawpaws and put them in your pocket,
Picking up pawpaws and put them in your pocket,
Way down yonder in the pawpaw patch.

Music Expansion

Encourage children to join in an activity by singing a child's name instead of *Johnny*. A sample verse might look like the following.

Where, oh where is dear little Aaron?
Where, oh where is dear little Rosa?
Where, oh where is dear little Justin?
Come and join us for our circle time.

Invite children to play a hide-and-seek game with the first verse of this song. Encourage children to cover their eyes while one child hides. When that child is hidden, invite the other children to search. When the child is found, sing the song and substitute the child's name for Johnny. Then change the last line to indicate where the child was found.

Invite children to make up actions for the song. They might also suggest new action phrases to be used such as jumping over pawpaws forward and backward. Suggest that children demonstrate the actions they mention.

Themes

Friends
Growing Things
Position Words

Featured Book

Growing Vegetable Soup by Lois Ehlert

Curriculum Integration

Choose activities from the following curriculum areas that fit your teaching style and the needs and interests of the children.

Science

Ask children what else might grow in a patch or garden such as cabbages, carrots, and strawberries. Help children learn that there are different ways to pick fruits and vegetables. For example, carrots would be pulled and potatoes would be dug. If a small garden area is available, help children plant some vegetables that grow quickly such as leaf lettuce or radishes.

Explain that *pawpaw* is another name for the fruit papaya. Bring in papaya and other fresh fruits and vegetables. Invite children to compare and contrast how the fruits and vegetables look and feel. Then cut the fruits and vegetables so children can observe the insides. Suggest they look at the colors and the seeds and smell them. Then invite children to taste the fruits and vegetables and compare the tastes.

Read *Growing Vegetable Soup* to children. Discuss the things plants need to grow and how they are harvested. Then read the recipe on the back of the book. Invite children to choose an ingredient to bring from home to make vegetable soup. (Use another recipe if you wish.) Encourage children to help with the preparation, serving, and cleanup. Children will enjoy identifying the vegetables as they eat the soup.

Math

Invite children to make a graph of the fruits and vegetables they tasted in Science. Write the names of the fruits and vegetables at the bottom of a sheet of graph paper and encourage children to place their initials above the ones they liked. Then talk about the results of the graph. Which fruit or vegetable was liked the most? the least? Did children like more fruits or more vegetables?

Provide seeds for children to sort or seriate. Encourage children to use words such as *larger, smaller, thinner,* and *thicker*.

Set up a flannel board in the math area. Provide a felt child and a felt "pawpaw patch." Encourage children to use position words such as *next to, under, over, in,* or *behind* as they sing the first verse of the song and manipulate the pieces on the flannel board.

Art

Offer children a variety of seeds and invite them to make a seed collage or a seed design.

Invite children to make fruit and vegetable prints. Help children cut fruits and vegetables in half. Then have children dip the cut ends of the fruits and vegetables into a shallow pan of paint. Encourage them to press the fruits and vegetables on sheets of paper to make designs. Children might want to use the dried prints as place mats for lunch.

Reading/Writing

Read *Growing Vegetable Soup*. Ask children to name other things they could grow such as a flower bouquet or a peanut butter and jelly sandwich. Make a list on chart paper of the children's suggestions and of all the items they would need to grow for each suggestion.

Invite children to write a book called *Where, Oh Where Is Johnny?* Suggest each child draw a picture of where Johnny might be. Then encourage children to dictate or write something about their pictures. Bind the pictures together to make the book. Display the book as the children sing new verses to the song.

Social Studies

Arrange to visit a commercial garden or a garden at a private home. Encourage children to ask questions of the gardener such as why the gardener has a garden. How does the gardener take care of the garden? What does the gardener do with the harvest from the garden?

Related Literature

Growing Vegetable Soup by Lois Ehlert. A father and child share the simple joy of planting, watering, and watching seeds grow in the family garden. Harcourt, 1987.

Planting a Rainbow by Lois Ehlert. Bold and exuberant pictures show the planting of a family garden. Bulbs, seeds, and seedlings grow into a brilliant rainbow of colorful flowers that are picked and carried home. And next year, a rainbow can grow all over again. Harcourt, 1988.

A Seed Is a Promise by Claire Merrill. This is a science book for young readers that explores the fascinating world of seeds, how they are made, and how they make new plants. Scholastic, 1990.

Vegetable Soup by Jeanne Modesitt. Elsie and Theodore are two very fussy bunnies until they run out of carrots and discover a whole world of new foods. Macmillan, 1988.

Pop Goes the Weasel

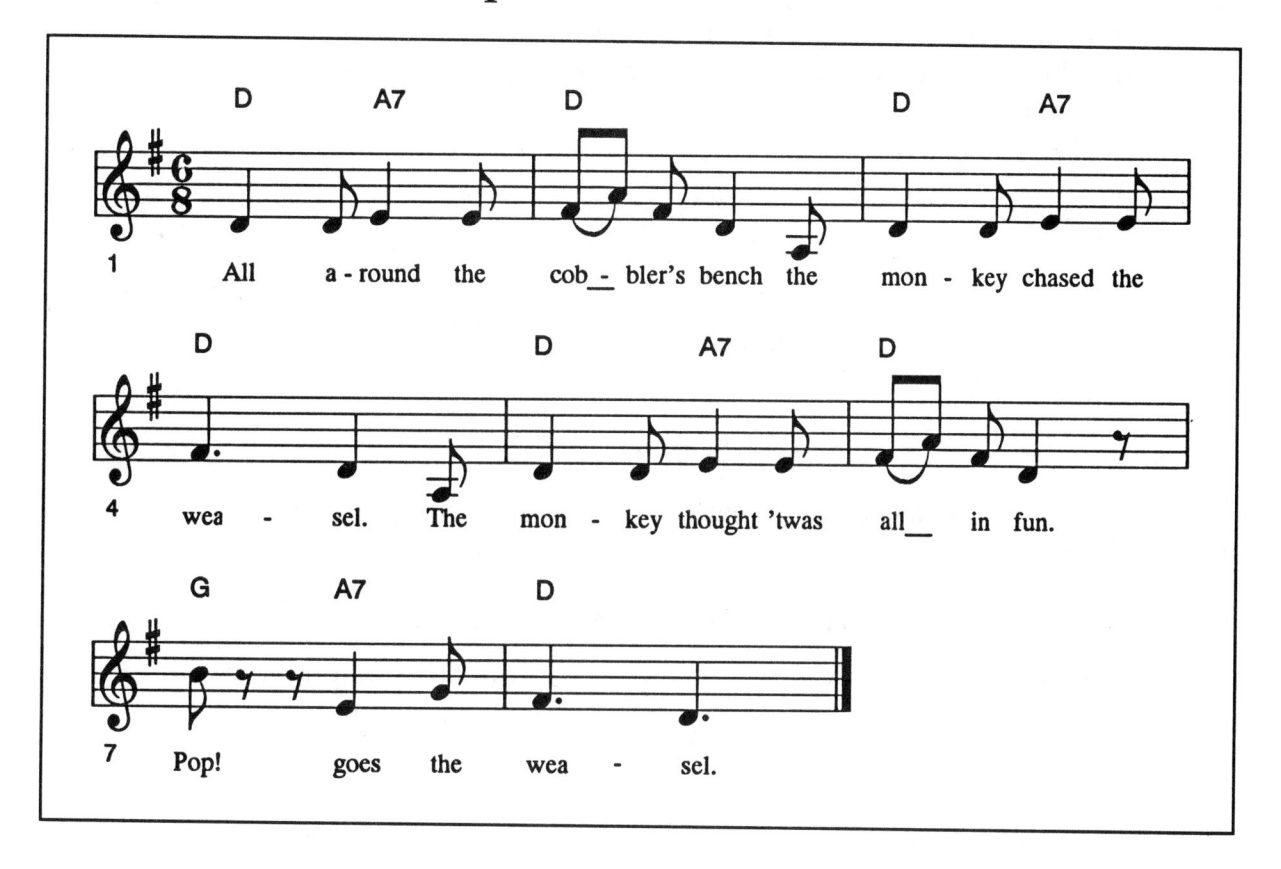

All around the cobbler's bench the monkey chased the weasel. The monkey thought 'twas all in fun. Pop! goes the weasel.

Music Expansion

Invite children to play a game with this song. First explain that a *cobbler* is a person who mends or makes shoes and a *cobbler's bench* is where the cobbler works. Ask children to sit in a circle and pretend to hammer on a cobbler's bench. Have one child pretend to be the weasel. Sing the song with the children as the weasel walks around the circle. On the word *pop,* the weasel taps another child (the monkey) on the shoulder. The monkey chases the weasel around the circle until the weasel arrives back at the monkey's spot and sits down. The monkey then becomes the weasel and the game continues.

Have children pass a ball, beanbag, or balloon around the circle while singing. On the word *pop,* the child holding the object tosses it to someone else. Vary the tempo of the song. Sing it slowly, then faster and faster.

Suggest children crouch down and pop up on the word *pop*.

Ask children to think of other animals to sing about instead of the monkey and the weasel. They might choose to move like these animals as they sing.

Themes
Animals
Clothing
Community Helpers

Featured Book
The Elves and the Shoemaker retold by Freya Littledale

Curriculum Integration
Choose activities from the following curriculum areas that fit your teaching style and the needs and interests of the children.

Science
Have an animal-awareness table in the science area. Provide pictures and picture books telling about weasels and different types of monkeys. Help children discover facts about these animals.

On a science table, place shoes made from different materials such as leather, satin, canvas, suede, and plastic. Encourage children to handle the shoes and talk about the textures using words such as *smooth*, *rough*, *soft*, and *hard*.

Math
Have children make a graph showing different kinds of shoes children in the class are wearing such as slip-ons, cowboy boots, sneakers, or sandals. Talk about the graph.

Point out that shoes come in pairs. Explain that *pair* means two of something. (If necessary, further explain that a pair of pants has two legs and a pair of scissors has two blades.) Invite children to count by twos the number of shoes in the room. Have them sit in a line on the floor. Help them count by telling them to say the first number (one) to themselves as you point to the first shoe. Then have them say the next number (two) aloud. Continue in this manner until all the shoes are counted.

Have children put one of their shoes in a pile in the middle of the circle. Invite each child to pick a shoe that isn't his or hers. Encourage children to look at the other children's shoes to find the mates and return the shoes to their owners.

Art

Invite children to make aluminum foil prints of their shoes. Place a folded towel on the floor and cover it with a 12" x 12" piece of foil. Have each child press his or her foot onto the foil and carefully lift it off to reveal the impression of the shoe. Place the impressions on a bulletin board and have children talk about the similarities and differences.

Read *The Elves and the Shoemaker* to children. Talk about the different shoes the elves make. Provide different shoe shapes made from oak tag. Have children choose a shape, trace it onto paper, and then create an interesting shoe. Suggest they use markers or crayons, construction paper scraps, ribbons, sequins, or other collage materials to add details to their shoes.

Reading/Writing

Read *The Elves and the Shoemaker*. Ask children what they think happens to the elves after they take their new clothes and return to the woods. Invite children to write a class story. Have children take turns creating sentences or phrases. Write their responses on a large sheet of chart paper. Encourage children to continue until they decide the story is finished. (Read the story at intervals to remind children what has already been dictated.) Then read the final story to them. Encourage children to illustrate the story. Display the story and illustrations in a prominent place.

Encourage children to talk about things that come in pairs. Write children's responses on chart paper. Then have each child choose an item on the list and draw a picture of it. Suggest children dictate or write something about their pictures. Bind the pictures together to make a book and add it to the class library.

Social Studies

Invite children to look at different types of shoes such as ballet shoes, cowboy boots, flippers, or hiking boots. Talk about who might wear each type of shoe and why they might need that particular type. Add the shoes to the dress-up area. (Ask parents to donate old shoes.)

Find examples or pictures of shoes from different areas of the world. If possible, add some examples to the dress-up area.

Remind children that the cobbler in the story made shoes. Discuss with children other jobs that are related to clothing such as tailors, seamstresses, hat makers (milliners), and salespeople.

Related Literature

Caps for Sale by Esphyr Slobodkina. This delightful children's classic is about a peddler of caps who runs into trouble when a pack of monkeys steals his wares. HarperCollins, 1947.

The Elves and the Shoemaker retold by Freya Littledale. Tiny elves help a poor shoemaker become rich. Scholastic, 1975.

Shoes by Elizabeth Winthrop. A survey of the many kinds of shoes in the world concludes that the best of all are the perfect, natural shoes that are your feet. HarperCollins, 1986.

Whose Shoes Are These? by Ron Roy. Text and photographs describe the appearance and function of almost twenty types of shoes, including work boots, snowshoes, and basketball sneakers. Houghton Mifflin, 1988.

Ring Around the Rosy

Ring a-round the ro-sy, pock-et full of po-sies. Ash-es, ash-es, we all fall down!

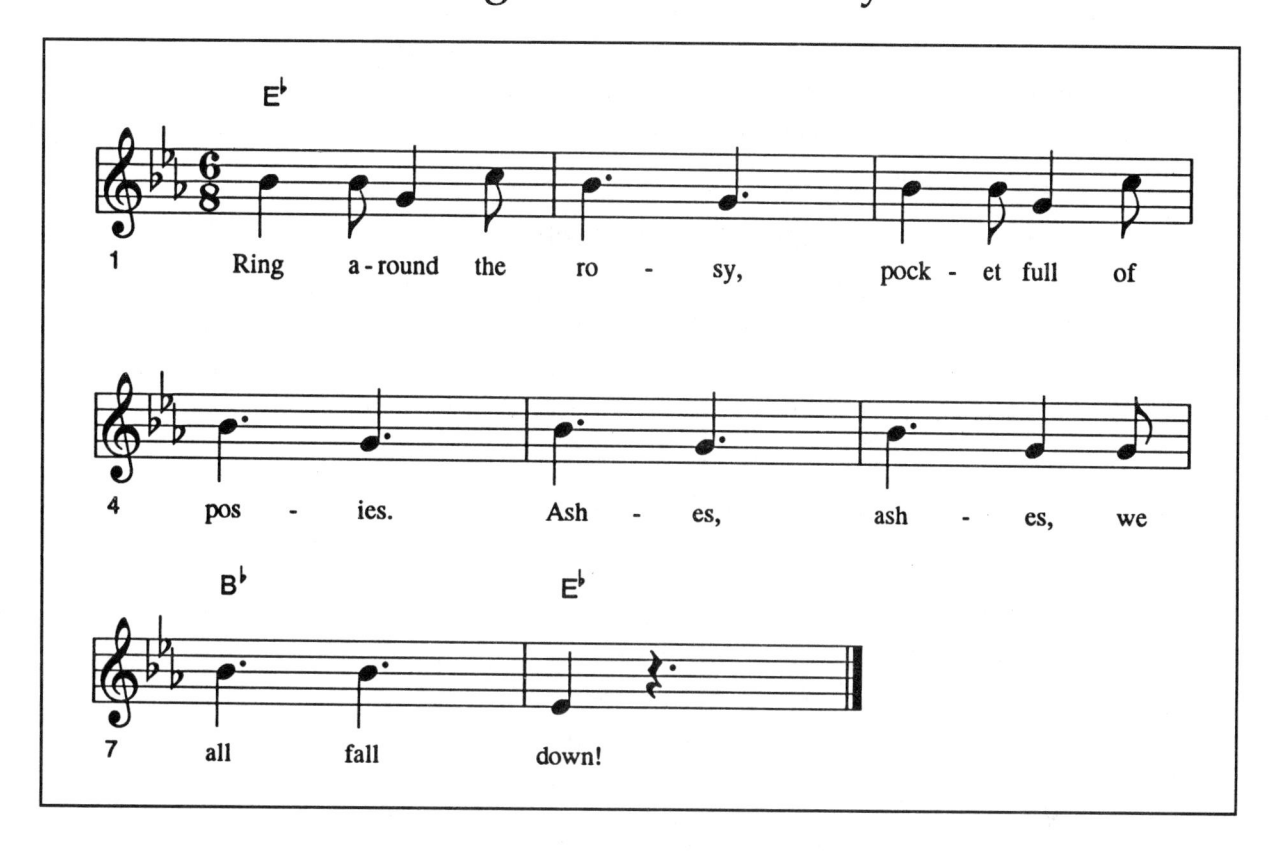

Music Expansion

Invite children to hold hands in a circle and move in one direction until the words *all fall down* are sung. Then suggest that everyone sit down on the floor.

Instead of singing *we all fall down*, sing *we all jump up, we all turn around,* or *we all clap our hands*. Ask children to make other suggestions.

Provide a parachute or large sheet. Have children hold onto the edges of the parachute or sheet as they sing and walk in a circle. On the words *all fall down*, suggest children raise the parachute or sheet high over their heads, duck under it, and sit down as the the parachute or sheet falls over them.

Invite children to choose a friend to hold hands with as they circle and sing.

Have each child hold a beanbag and substitute the word *beanbag* for *ashes*. Have children suggest things to do with the beanbags.

...beanbags, beanbags, touch the ground.

...beanbags, beanbags, toss to a friend.

...beanbags, beanbags, behind your back.

...beanbags, beanbags, under your foot.

...beanbags, beanbags, in front of your nose.

...beanbags, beanbags, on your head.

Themes

Friends
Position Words
Shapes

Featured Book

Rosie's Walk by Pat Hutchins

Curriculum Integration

Choose activities from the following curriculum areas that fit your teaching style and the needs and interests of the children.

Science

Read *Rosie's Walk*. Then help children set up an obstacle course. They might walk between two chairs, crawl under a table, and climb over a pillow. Encourage children to use position words to explain how to move through the course.

Help children make a bubble mixture. Have them measure 2 cups of liquid dish detergent, 6 cups of water, and 3/4 cup light corn syrup into a large plastic container. (A plastic gallon milk jug can also be used.) Shake well and let stand at least four hours. Store in the refrigerator to extend the life of the bubbles.

Next have children make various sizes of rings from regular pipe cleaners or florist wire. Invite them to use the rings and the bubble mixture to make bubbles. Encourage children to talk about the differences in the bubbles that come from the various rings. Suggest that interested children make other shapes from pipe cleaners and use those with bubbles. Have them compare the bubbles that come from all the shapes.

Math

Invite children to "measure" things in the room such as tables, chairs, or bookshelves. Have two children hold hands and make a ring around the object. If two children are not enough, have children join the pair one at a time until they form a ring. Then invite children to count how many children it took to make a ring around the object. Write the results on chart paper.

Make or purchase a ring toss game for children. (A dowel set in a wooden base and canning jar rings work well.) Place a masking-tape line on the floor a short distance from the base. Then invite each child to toss five rings over the dowel. Have children graph the number of rings that went over the dowel. Encourage children to practice and try again. Have children graph the results several times to see their progress.

Ask children what shape they think of when they see a ring. Encourage them to look around the room and find similar shapes such as a clock, a ball, or the letter O.

Art

Provide children with dark-colored construction paper. Invite them to "catch" bubbles on the construction paper. (See Science.) Help children notice the designs created when the bubbles pop.

Offer children different sizes and shapes of construction paper and glue. Invite them to glue the shapes to another sheet of construction paper to make a picture or design.

Reading/Writing

Read *Rosie's Walk* aloud to children. Invite children to write a group story about Rosie when she visits a friend outside the barnyard. Help children decide on a setting such as in the forest, in a city, or at school. Encourage them to use position words as they tell where Rosie goes on her walk.

Social Studies

Give children directions using position words. For example, ask them to walk around the table, stand next to a friend, hide behind the teacher, and go back to the starting spot. Encourage children to do the same activity with a friend.

Invite children to go for a walk around the neighborhood. Encourage them to look for shapes as they look at the surroundings.

Related Literature

If You Look Around You by Fulvio Testa. The wonders of geometry and shapes are explored in objects all around us. Dial, 1987.

Look Around! A Book About Shapes by Leonard Everett Fisher. Basic geometric shapes are presented in familiar settings. Penguin, 1989.

over, under & through by Tana Hoban. Photographs demonstrate the spatial concepts expressed in twelve words such as *around*, *across*, *between*, *against*, and *behind*. Atheneum, 1973.

Rosie's Walk by Pat Hutchins. Rosie the hen goes out for a walk around the barnyard and unknowingly outwits a fox. Macmillan, 1971.

Row, Row, Row Your Boat

C
1 Row, row, row your boat gent - ly down the
4 stream. Mer- ri - ly, mer- ri - ly, mer - ri - ly, mer- ri - ly,
G7 C
7 life is but a dream.

Music Expansion

Invite children to pretend to row a boat while singing. Then sing the song varying the tempo. Have children adjust their rowing to match the song's tempo.

Encourage children to brainstorm other forms of transportation and make up rhymes to complete the song. Verses might include

Ride, ride, ride the train
Gently down the track.
Merrily, merrily, merrily, merrily.
When will it come back?

Pedal, pedal, pedal your bike
Gently 'round the block.
Merrily, merrily, merrily, merrily.
Watch out! Don't hit that rock!

Themes

Bodies of Water
Transportation

Featured Book

Harbor by Donald Crews

Curriculum Integration

Choose activities from the following curriculum areas that fit your teaching style and the needs and interests of the children.

Science

Fill the water table and then invite children to construct boats from wood, aluminum foil, or other materials. Have children place their boats in the water and use their hands to move the water gently. Ask them to observe how the boats move. Then have children churn the water vigorously. What happens to the boats?

Invite children to brainstorm a list of bodies of water. Write the children's responses on chart paper. Next read *Harbor* aloud to children. Then ask them to find pictures of boats and ships in old magazines and cut them out. Talk about the pictures. Encourage children to decide on which body or bodies of water each boat or ship might be found. Glue the pictures onto a large sheet of mural paper and write the body or bodies of water the children choose next to the pictures.

Math

Have children place their boats in a water table. (See Science.) Provide pennies or washers. Suggest children take turns placing pennies or washers, one at a time, on their boats until the boats sink. When each boat sinks, have the child count the number of pennies or washers and write the number and his or her initials at the bottom of a sheet of graph paper. Then ask the child to color in the corresponding number of squares above the number. When the graph is finished, talk about the results.

DM 4	WM 1	GBI 3	KN 2

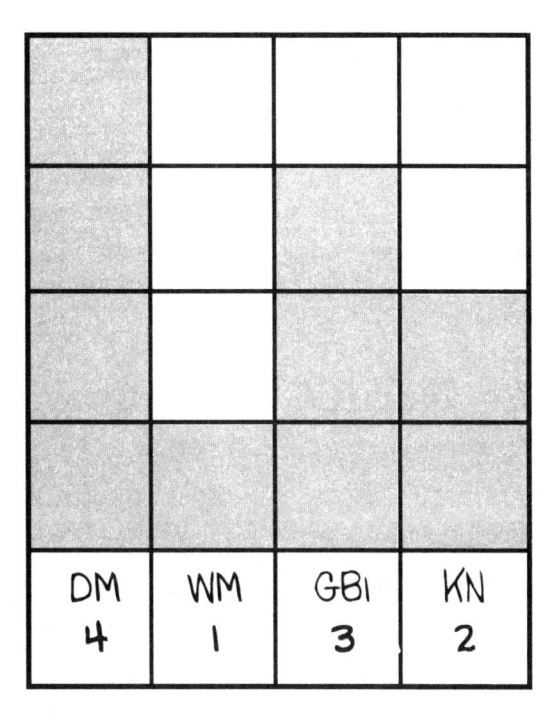

Art

Invite children to form small groups and create boats using large cardboard boxes. Suggest that each group paint a box or decorate it with collage materials. Explain that a boat usually has a name that means something to the owner. Encourage each group to give its boat a name.

Have children use crayons to make pictures of boats. Then provide water-thinned blue paint. Encourage children to use broad paintbrushes and lightly brush the blue paint over their pictures. Help children notice that the paint sticks to the paper but not to the crayon.

Reading/Writing

Read *Harbor* to children. Talk about the boats, where they may have come from, and where they might be going. Then invite children to cut out magazine pictures of boats and glue the pictures onto sheets of paper. Encourage each child to write or dictate a story about the pictured boat. They might want to include where the boat is going, where it came from, why it's in the harbor, and who is on it. Display the pictures and stories on a bulletin board or bind the pages together to make a book.

Social Studies

Visit a boat sales display or a marina. Suggest children compare the various kinds of boats they see.

Ask children to talk about uses for boats. They might suggest that boats are a way to travel, a means of moving things from one place to another, or a way to have fun.

Related Literature

Big City Port by Betsy Maestro and Ellen Del Vecchio. A colorful panorama of liners, cargo ships, tugs, and freighters float on the waters of a big city port. Macmillan, 1984.

Boats by Anne Rockwell. Colorful boats of all shapes and sizes float through waters in this delightful introduction to boats. Dutton, 1985.

Harbor by Donald Crews. Various kinds of boats come and go in a busy harbor. Greenwillow, 1982.

Little Toot by Hardy Gramatky. A little tugboat in New York harbor wishes for the same adventure and work that his father and grandfather have. Putnam, 1978.

Who Sank the Boat? by Pamela Allen. The reader is invited to guess who causes the boat to sink when five animal friends of varying sizes decide to go for a row. Putnam, 1985.

Shalom Chavarim

(musical score with lyrics: "Shalom, chavarim, shalom, chavarim, shalom, shalom. L'hitra-ot, l'hitra-ot, shalom, shalom.")

Music Expansion

Explain that *shalom* is a Hebrew word that means *hello, good-bye*, or *peace*; *chavarim* means *children*; and *l'hitra-ot* means *until later*. This song can be sung as both a hello song and a good-bye song.

Israeli dancing can be simplified and taught to young children. Since the traditional grapevine step is too difficult for most children, suggest that children walk in a circle holding hands while singing "Shalom Chavarim." When the words *l'hitra-ot* are sung, encourage the children to clap their hands first over their right shoulders and then over their left shoulders. On the the words *Shalom, shalom*, have them hold hands and walk around the circle again.

Themes

Cultures
Friends
Holidays
Shapes

Featured Book

It Could Always Be Worse retold by Margot Zemach

Curriculum Integration

Choose activities from the following curriculum areas that fit your teaching style and the needs and interests of the children.

Science

Remind children that the song is sung in Hebrew and Hebrew is the language spoken by Jewish people in the country of Israel. (Hebrew and Arabic are the two national languages of Israel.) Provide foods that are native to Israel such as figs, dates, olives, almonds, oranges, and grapes. Encourage children to handle the foods. Then help them cut up the fruits and crack the nuts. Invite children to smell and taste the foods and compare the flavors, textures, and aromas.

Invite children to make traditional Israeli sandwiches. Help children prepare felafel (fried chickpea balls) according to package directions and serve it in pita bread with lettuce. Felafel mix can be found in most health food stores or the foreign food section of most grocery stores.

Math

Show children an Israeli flag or a picture of one from an encyclopedia. Ask them what shapes and colors they see. (The white rectangular flag has a parallel bar, or rectangle, across the top and bottom. There is a star, the Star of David, in the center.) What shapes were used to make the star? Then provide craft sticks and invite children to make a star from two triangles. Some children may choose to make additional shapes with the sticks.

Show children a five-pointed star and a six-pointed star. Ask them how the stars are alike and how they are different. Ask children to count the points on the stars. Then encourage children to create sets of five or six items such as five blocks or six craft sticks.

Read *It Could Always Be Worse* aloud to children. Provide flannel board characters of the man, his wife, his mother, and his six children. Invite children to count how many people live in the man's house. Then add four chickens and ask children to count how many are in the man's house. Continue the activity by adding one rooster, one goose, a goat, and a cow. Pause after each new animal is added and invite the children to count. Then take away all the animals and count how many people are left in the man's house. Invite children to do this activity with a friend. Others may choose to sequence the order in which the man brought the animals into the house.

Art

Provide children with triangles and rectangles of various sizes, colors, and textures. Then invite them to make collages or designs by gluing them onto wallpaper samples or onto construction paper.

Display the United States flag and an Israeli flag. Explain that most countries have national flags. Then invite children to create a flag for a new country. Encourage them to use a variety of art materials. Suggest that children give their new countries names. Display the flags on a bulletin board or wall.

Reading/Writing

Read *It Could Always Be Worse*. Explain that this story is a folktale. A *folktale* is a story that has been told orally over the years by parents to children, who then tell the story to their children, and on through the generations. Ask children how they think the man feels at the beginning of the story. How does he feel after he brings all the animals into the house? How is the house different at the end of the story than at the beginning? Encourage children to discuss and give reasons for their responses.

Contact a local synagogue in order to borrow some books in Hebrew. Show children how the books open from the left instead of from the right. Also point out that people read and write Hebrew from right to left while people read and write English left to right.

Provide children with sheets of drawing paper. Invite each child to draw a self-portrait. When the pictures are completed, bind the pages into a book with a blank page after each child's picture. Suggest children write their names on the blank page after their pictures. Encourage children to look through the book and write or dictate something about each of the other children in the book on their appropriate pages.

Ask children how else they might greet a friend besides saying *hello*. Write children's responses on chart paper. Do the same for *good-bye*. Post the charts in the language area and encourage children to add to the list often.

Social Studies

On a globe or world map, show where Israel is. Then point out the country the children live in. Ask children to compare the size and location of the two countries.

Invite someone who speaks Hebrew to come into the classroom and demonstrate Hebrew writing and language. Suggest that the guest teach children a few words in Hebrew. Local synagogues, language centers, or universities or colleges would be community resources.

Point out that Hebrew-speaking people celebrate holidays that may be different to children. Invite a parent or someone from the community to come in and tell a little about the holidays. The holidays might include

> Hanukkah, The Festival of Lights, is celebrated in December. During Hanukkah gifts are exchanged and contributions are given to the poor. Every night for eight nights an additional candle is lit in a special candelabrum called a *menorah*. The candles are lit using a special candle called a *shammash*.
>
> Sukkot, a harvest festival, is in the fall. The participants eat meals in a specially constructed roofless building called a *succah*.

Passover, commemorating the exodus from Egypt, is in the spring. There is a huge meal called a *seder* that includes a religious service and foods with symbolic meanings.

Rosh Hashanah, the New Year, is in the fall. It is an important holiday. People traditionally eat apples dipped in honey to wish everyone a sweet year.

Yom Kippur, the Day of Atonement, is in the fall. It is the most important holiday. Adults fast for 24 hours to atone for their sins of the past year. Children are encouraged to apologize for any wrongdoings during the year and think of ways to help. It is followed at sundown the next evening by a big meal called a *breakfast*.

For more information on these holidays, contact a local synagogue or the public library.

Invite children and parents to talk about various holidays they celebrate in their homes. Provide a place for children to display pictures of holiday activities.

Related Literature

Count Your Way Through Israel by Jim Haskins. Young readers count their way through Israel in Hebrew, one of Israel's two official languages, and learn about this diverse Middle Eastern country. Carolrhoda, 1990.

It Could Always Be Worse retold by Margot Zemach. A wise Rabbi advises a large family about living harmoniously in a small hut. Farrar, Straus and Giroux, 1976.

Just Enough Is Plenty by Barbara Diamond Goldin. With Hanukkah about to begin, Maika is worried because her family is so poor. When a stranger comes to the door, her generous family cannot turn him away. Viking, 1988.

Rosie and Michael by Judith Viorst. Rosie and Michael's friendship is big enough for jokes, for sharing possessions, for aiding each other in emergencies, and even for being mad once in a while. Macmillan, 1974.

The Treasure by Uri Shulevitz. A poor man, inspired by a recurring dream, journeys to a far city to look for a treasure. There he is advised to return home and find it. Farrar, Straus and Giroux, 1979.

She'll Be Coming 'Round the Mountain

She'll be coming 'round the mountain when she comes. [Toot!] [Toot!] She'll be coming 'round the mountain when she comes. [Toot!] [Toot!] She'll be coming 'round the mountain, she'll be coming 'round the mountain, she'll be coming 'round the mountain when she comes. [Toot!] [Toot!]

Additional verses

She'll be drivin' six white horses . . . Whoa back! *(Pull on pretend reins.)*

We will all go out to greet her . . . Hi, babe! *(Wave hello.)*

We will kill the old red rooster . . . Hack! Hack! *(Chop arm.)*

We will all have chicken and dumplings . . . Yum! Yum! *(Rub tummy.)*

She will wear her red pajamas . . . Scratch! Scratch! *(Scratch side of body.)*

She will have to sleep with grandma . . . Snore! Snore! *(Pretend to sleep.)*

Music Expansion

Provide felt shapes to place on a flannel board as cues for children. Suggested shapes include

> a girl, a mountain, or a train
> a horse
> a hand (waving)
> a rooster
> a bowl (of food)
> red long johns
> a bed

Encourage children to use instruments to represent each sound. A whistle could be the "toot toot," and rhythm sticks could be "whoa back." Have children suggest sounds and actions for each verse. Explain that the first verse implies that the person is coming by train. Then invite children to form a train and travel around the room while singing. Suggest children take turns being the engine and caboose as each verse is sung.

Themes

Family
Transportation

Featured Book

Things That Go by Anne Rockwell

Curriculum Integration

Choose activities from the following curriculum areas that fit your teaching style and the needs and interests of the children.

Art

Share the book *Things That Go* with children. Invite each child to choose a form of transportation that is shown in the book. Then have children pretend that they are using that form of transportation to go somewhere. Encourage them to use a variety of art materials and create a picture of the place they would go and whom they would visit.

Point out that some of the things that go in the book are not forms of transportation. For example, croquet balls, rubber balls, and cultivators all move, but they don't provide transportation. Invite children to watch marbles or small balls move as they make colorful designs. Have each child place a sheet of paper in the lid of a shoe box or on a tray with sides. Next have children dip marbles or small balls into tempera paint and place them on the papers. Suggest children gently tilt the lids or trays back and forth. Some children may want to use several marbles that have been dipped in different colors. Display the designs on a wall or bulletin board.

Provide children with shoe boxes and invite them to create a form of transportation for the future. Make available a variety of art materials, fabric scraps, and other collage materials. Encourage children to dictate or write something about their new forms of transportation on note cards. Display the new inventions and note cards on a table in a prominent area of the room.

Science

Remind children that the family and friends in the song had chicken and dumplings for a meal. Invite children to help make chicken and dumplings for lunch. (Supervise children around boiling broth.)

Chicken and Dumplings

Ingredients

2 16-ounce cans chicken broth
2 5-ounce cans cooked chicken
1 15-ounce can mixed vegetables
1 cup flour
2 teaspoons baking powder
1/2 teaspoon salt
2 tablespoons salad oil
1/2 cup milk

Utensils

3-quart saucepan
measuring cups
measuring spoons
mixing bowl
mixing spoon
tablespoon

Place chicken broth, chicken, and vegetables in a saucepan. Place over heat and bring to a boil. Combine flour, baking powder, and salt in a bowl. Add oil to milk. Add to dry ingredients all at once. Stir until just moistened. Drop from tablespoon on top of liquid in saucepan. Cover tightly and return to boil. Reduce heat (don't lift cover). Simmer 12 to 15 minutes. Makes 10 dumplings.

Point out that each verse of the song suggests a sound that might be heard, for example, the sounds of the train, the horses, the rooster, and Grandma snoring. Make an audiotape of everyday sounds such as a car horn, someone snoring, or a washing machine. Invite children to close their eyes and listen to the tape. Ask them to identify the sounds they think they hear.

Remind children that the person in the song came around the mountain on a train and then traveled by stagecoach (". . . driving six white horses . . ."). Show children pictures of an old steam engine and a stagecoach. Ask children to brainstorm a list of things that make it possible to get from one place to another. Write children's responses on chart paper. Encourage them to add to the list at any time.

Math

Invite children to sequence the felt shapes suggested in Music Expansion in the same order that they appear in the song.

Suggest children make "trains" using stringing beads and laces. Encourage each child to string five or six beads on a lace and then create the same pattern on a second lace. Some children may want to create the pattern starting at the opposite end. For example, if a blue bead was the last to be added to the first lace, then it would be the first to be added on the second lace.

Read *Things That Go*. Discuss with children the variety of transportation forms shown in the book. Then invite children to make a graph of the different forms of transportation they have ridden on. List various forms such as cars, buses, skateboards, planes, and rocket ships across the bottom of a sheet of graph paper. Next say one of the forms and have children who have been on that form stand. Choose a child who is not standing to count the children standing and color in the correct number of squares above that form of transportation. Then talk about the results of the graph with children.

Reading/Writing

Invite children to create a modern or futuristic song about traveling. Ask them where they will be coming from. What will they be driving? Whom would they visit? What would they do while visiting? Have children contribute new ideas, sounds, and motions as they sing the new songs.

Read *Things That Go*. Encourage children to revise or add to the previous list of modes of transportation they made. (See Science.)

Social Studies

Help children plan a visitors' day. Encourage each child to invite a member of their family or a friend to come and visit the classroom. Suggest they plan a tour of the classroom for the guests, refreshments, decorations, and entertainment.

Explain to children that this song was written about a time long ago when pioneers were traveling west to places like California. Set up an "Old West" table in the social studies area and display items related to the time period such as toy stagecoaches and trains; pictures of towns, people, and transportation used; books about the theme; and items that children might wish to add.

Help children set up a train station or stagecoach stop in the dramatic play area. Discuss with them what might be needed. Suggestions might include chairs to represent the seats on a train, in a stagecoach, or in a waiting area; a desk for a ticket window; play money; and paper for tickets and signs.

Related Literature

Airport by Byron Barton. Describes and pictures what happens from the time an airplane passenger arrives at an airport and boards an airplane until the plane is in the air. HarperCollins, 1982.

First Flight by David McPhail. On his first plane trip, a little boy is a model passenger, but his toy bear, now grown to enormous size, is a terror in the aisles. Little, 1987.

Freight Train by Donald Crews. Brief text and illustrations trace the journey of a colorful train as it goes through tunnels, by cities, and over trestles. Greenwillow, 1978.

Things That Go by Anne Rockwell. Movable objects are brightly illustrated in this informative book for young readers. Dutton, 1986.

Things That Go: A Traveling Alphabet Book by Seymour Reit. Text and illustrations introduce vehicles from A (ambulance) to Z (zeppelin). Bantam, 1990.

There Was an Old Lady

I know an old lady who swallowed a fly. I don't know why she swallowed a fly. Perhaps she'll die. There was an old lady who swallowed a spider that wriggled and jiggled and tickled inside her. She swallowed the spider to catch the fly.

150

There Was an Old Lady (continued)

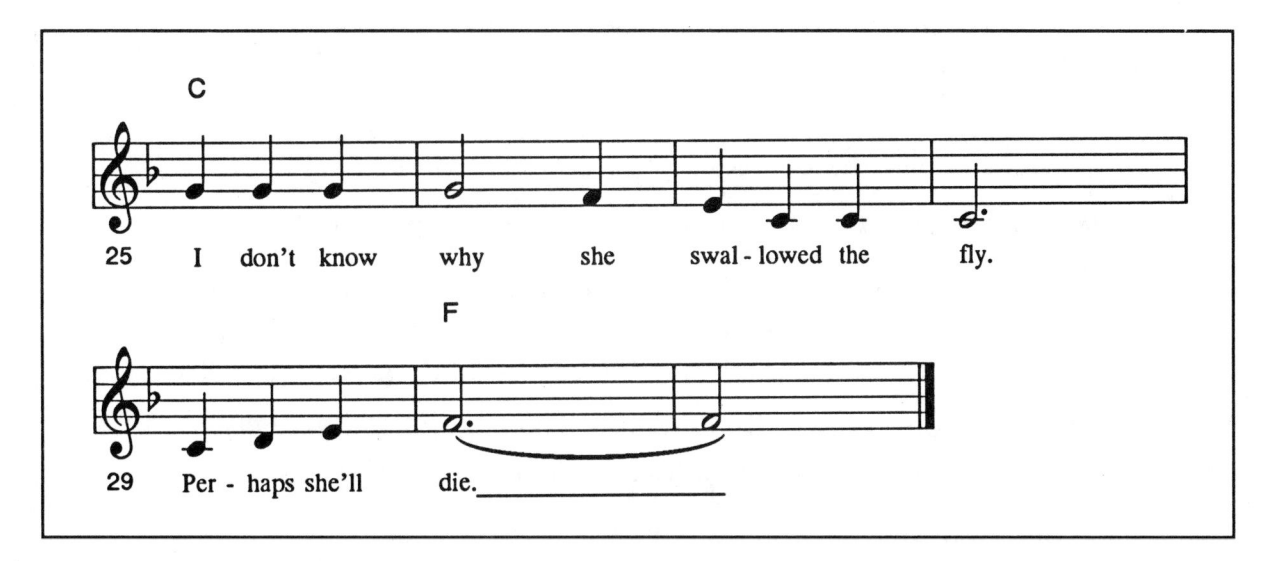

(musical notation: measures 25–29)

25 I don't know why she swal-lowed the fly.
29 Per-haps she'll die.

Additional verses

I know an old lady who swallowed a bird.
How absurd to swallow a bird.
She swallowed the bird to catch the spider
That wriggled and jiggled and tickled inside her.
She swallowed the spider to catch the fly.
I don't know why she swallowed the fly.
Perhaps she'll die.

. . . a cat.
Imagine that to swallow a cat . . .

. . . a dog.
What a hog to swallow a dog . . .

. . . a goat.
She just opened her throat, and in walked the goat . . .

. . . a cow.
I don't know how she swallowed that cow . . .

. . . a horse.
She's dead, of course.

Music Expansion

Invite children to make up new verses for the song. For example, they might suggest the following verse.

> . . . a mouse.
> It came into her house, so she swallowed the mouse.

Provide children with felt pictures as cues to the verses in the song.

Make an Old Lady puppet out of a paper bag or sock and attach a cloth or a paper bag for her body. Encourage children to drop plastic animals or cutouts of animals into the bag as the song is sung.

Substitute one of the children's names instead of the words *old lady*. For example, you might sing one of the following verses.

> I once saw Melissa swallow a bunny.
> When she was done, she felt really funny. . . .
>
> I once saw young Mike swallow a frog.
> He jumped right up and sat on a log. . . .

Themes

Animals
Food/Nutrition
Health
Insects

Featured Book

I Know a Lady by Charlotte Zolotow

Curriculum Integration

Choose activities from the following curriculum areas that fit your teaching style and the needs and interests of the children.

Science

This is a great song to use when studying a food chain. Invite children to write new verses that will put the food chain in the correct order. For example, an owl eats a mouse that ate some corn, or a big fish eats a little fish that ate a littler fish that ate a bug.

Ask children what they think the lady should have eaten instead of the fly. What do they think she might eat for breakfast? for lunch? for dinner? Then invite children to cut food pictures from magazines that they think would make a good, healthy meal. Have them glue the pictures to a paper plate. Encourage interested children to make a paper-plate picture for each meal.

Math

Invite children to count how many things the old lady ate. Or place pictures of all of the items on the flannel board. Sing the song and as the old lady eats something, pause and ask a child to remove that picture from the flannel board. Invite the children to count how many items are left each time.

Provide the felt pictures and flannel board used in Music Expansion and suggest children sequence them in the order they appear in the song.

Art

Set out juice cans, paper towel rolls, pom-poms, googly eyes, pipe cleaners, yarn, fabric and paper scraps, and glue. Invite children to create creatures. When the creatures are completed, encourage children to dictate or write something about their creatures. Ask children if they think the old lady would swallow their creatures. Why or why not?

Read *I Know a Lady* to children. Ask children how old they think the lady in the book is. How did they come to their conclusions? Then point out that the illustrations were done in pen and watercolor. Provide children with paper, fine-line pens, watercolors, and paintbrushes. Encourage them to draw and paint pictures of older people they know. When the pictures are finished, suggest that each child dictate or write something about the person in his or her picture. Display the pictures and descriptions on an Older Friends bulletin board.

Reading/Writing

Read *I Know a Lady*. Ask children what they think they will be like when they are older. What will they be doing? Who will be their friends? Then have children draw pictures of themselves as older adults. Suggest they dictate or write something about themselves as an older adult. Encourage volunteers to share their pictures and descriptions with the class.

Social Studies

Arrange for children to visit a care center or senior citizens' home. Have children draw pictures for the seniors. Suggest that they choose several of their favorite songs to perform for the group.

Related Literature

The Crack-of-Dawn Walkers by Amy Hest. At the crack of dawn, Sadie and her grandfather take a walk to Emma's Bake Shop and then to Fabio's for a warm drink and some candy. Macmillan, 1984.

Emma by Wendy Desselman. Emma's visiting relatives give her a painting on her 72nd birthday that inspires her to begin a whole new life by becoming a painter herself. HarperCollins, 1985.

I Know a Lady by Charlotte Zolotow. Sally describes a loving and lovable lady in her neighborhood who grows flowers, waves to children, and bakes cookies for them. Greenwillow, 1984.

Music, Music for Everyone by Vera B. Williams. Grandma says Rosa's music makes her feel like a young girl again, and that is the beginning of Rosa's wonderful idea. Greenwillow, 1984.

A Special Trade by Sally Wittman. As years go by, a little girl is able to help an old man as he helped her when she was very young. HarperCollins, 1985.

Twinkle, Twinkle Little Star

Music Expansion

Invite children to sing as if they feel angry, sad, tired, frustrated, or happy. First suggest children make facial expressions and body movements that might accompany the feeling. Then have them sing the song to reflect the various emotions.

Invite children to play a hiding game. Hide one construction-paper star for each child in the room. Be sure that portions of the stars show. As children sing the song, have them search the room for the stars. Suggest that they sit down when they find a star.

Encourage children to create hand motions for the song.

Have children curl up and pretend they are stars sleeping. Sing the song and tap each child on the head. As they are tapped, suggest children "come out and twinkle" by standing up and singing the song.

Themes

Alphabet
Counting/Numbers
Night
Nursery Rhymes
Shapes

Featured Book

Grandfather Twilight by Barbara Berger

Curriculum Integration

Choose activities from the following curriculum areas that fit your teaching style and the needs and interests of the children.

Science

Read *Grandfather Twilight* to children. Point out that in the story Grandfather's pearl becomes the moon. Then ask children how they think stars came to be. What do they think stars are made of? Where do they think the stars go during the day? Write children's responses on chart paper.

Ask children what they think makes night and day different. Then invite children to make a list of things that happen during the day and a list of things that happen during the night. Post the lists in the science area.

Have children brainstorm a list of things that twinkle. Then invite them to bring items that twinkle from home. Display the items on a discovery table in the science area and encourage children to add to the items as they find new things that twinkle.

Math

Invite children to "fish" for stars. Make stars out of heavy paper, draw shapes or write numbers or letters on them, and attach a paper clip to each. Construct fishing poles out of dowels. Tie one end of a string to a dowel and the other end of the string to a magnet. Place the stars on the floor and have children use the magnet to "catch" the paper clip on the star. Make a set of cards to match the shapes, numbers, or letters on the the stars. Invite children to choose a card and then "fish" for the matching star.

Art

Suggest children make star gazers. Have children tape black paper over one end of paper tubes. Then suggest they use blunt needles to poke holes for stars in the black paper. To see the "night sky" in their tubes, suggest children face a window and hold the tubes up to their eyes.

Provide white chalk, white crayons, white paint, white fingerpaints, black or dark blue paper, and stick-on foil stars. Then invite children to create night pictures.

Reading/Writing

Read *Grandfather Twilight*. Talk with children about how, each night, Grandfather Twilight takes one pearl from a strand of pearls and walks to the edge of the sea. Then ask children what they think Grandmother Daylight might do. What kind of jewel might she have? What would it become? Suggest children draw pictures showing Grandmother Daylight. Encourage children to dictate or write a short story about Grandmother Daylight.

After reading *Grandfather Twilight*, invite children to compare the story to *Anansi the Spider* (the featured book for "The Eency Weency Spider"). Help children notice that each story gives an explanation for the creation of the moon. Encourage them to write and illustrate their own stories explaining how the moon came to be. Display the stories and illustrations in the language arts area.

Invite children to dictate or write about things they do at night. Then suggest they illustrate their stories. Compile the pages into a class book, *Things I Do at Night*. Place the book in the class library.

Social Studies

Help children plan a bedtime-reading day. Invite children to bring sleeping bags or blankets, pillows, and their favorite nighttime storybooks. Set aside an area where children can spread out their blankets and sleeping bags. Encourage them to curl up and read during free time. Suggest children talk about their books to each other and exchange books to read.

Host a Bedtime Story Hour. Plan an evening to invite families to bring their children to school in their pajamas with blankets and pillows. Arrange for a children's storyteller to come in and tell bedtime stories or read bedtime books to the families. (Often the children's librarian at the local public library is available for this.) Before the families leave, offer a bedtime snack of milk and cookies.

Related Literature

Goodnight Moon by Margaret Wise Brown. A little rabbit bids goodnight to each familiar thing in his room. HarperCollins, 1947.

Grandfather Twilight by Barbara Berger. At day's end, Grandfather Twilight walks in the forest to perform his task, bringing the miracle of night to the world. Putnam, 1984.

Night in the Country by Cynthia Rylant. Text and illustrations describe the sights and sounds of nighttime in the country. Macmillan, 1986.

Where Does the Sun Go at Night? by Mirra Ginsburg. A poetic fantasy that gives small questioners an imaginative and decidedly satisfying answer to a hard-to-answer question. Greenwillow, 1980.

The Wheels on the Bus

The wheels on the bus go 'round and 'round, 'round and 'round, 'round and 'round. The wheels on the bus go 'round and 'round, all through the town.

Additional verses

The money on the bus goes clink, clink, clink . . .

The driver on the bus says, "Move on back . . ."

The horn on the bus goes beep, beep, beep . . .

The wipers on the bus go swish, swish, swish . . .

The children on the bus go up and down . . .

The babies on the bus go, "Waa, waa, waa . . ."

The parents on the bus go, "Sh-sh-sh . . ."

Music Expansion

Ask children to make up other verses about a bus and its passengers. Some examples of verses might include

The door on the bus goes open and close . . .

The lights on the bus go on and off . . .

Ask children to brainstorm a list of other forms of transportation. Then encourage them to make up verses to go with some of the other transportation forms.

The wings on the plane go tilt, tilt, tilt . . .

The hooves on the horse go clip, clop, clop . . .

Help children think of instruments to use for sound effects. The money could be a triangle, and the horn could be a bike horn.

Themes

Position Words
Simple Machines
Transportation

Featured Book

Wheel Away! by Dayle Ann Dodds

Curriculum Integration

Choose activities from the following curriculum areas that fit your teaching style and the needs and interests of the children.

Science

Invite children to build ramps with blocks and experiment with speed. Provide toy vehicles, balls, or marbles. Encourage children to place two items at the top of their ramps and estimate which one will reach the bottom first. Suggest that they vary the steepness of the ramp to see how it affects the speed.

Read *Wheel Away!* to children. Encourage children to brainstorm a list of things that have wheels. Ask them why they think people need things with wheels. Then invite children to experiment to see how wheels help move things. First give children a box and some blocks. Have children push the empty box. Ask them if it was easy or hard to move the box. Then have children fill the box with blocks and try to move the box again. Ask them if it was easier or harder to move the block-filled box. Have children remove the blocks from the box. Next give children a mechanic's creeper or a skateboard. Have them place the empty box on the creeper or skateboard and fill the box with the blocks again. Suggest children push the creeper or skateboard to move the box. Ask children if the box was easier to move with or without the creeper or skateboard. Encourage them to give reasons for their answers.

Math

Line up children along one side of a school bus. Ask children to help count how many children long the bus is. (If a bus is not available, use a car.) Then invite children to use a piece of string to measure the length of the vehicle. Take the piece of string into the classroom and suggest children stretch the string to see if the vehicle would fit inside the room.

Provide magazine pictures of various transportation forms. Place a large sheet of mural paper on the lower part of a wall. Divide the paper into three sections. At the top of the first section, glue a picture of a road. At the top of the middle section, glue a picture of the sky. At the top of the last section, glue a picture of water. Then invite children to glue transportation pictures under the appropriate heading. Children might want to look through magazines for pictures of transportation to add to the mural.

Help children set up a bus station. Arrange two rows of chairs for seats on the bus. Place a picture, number, color, or shape on each seat. Have children pretend to be passengers. Have "tickets" that match the pictures, numbers, colors, or shapes used on the chairs. Then encourage the "passengers" to find the seats that match their tickets.

Art

Place construction-paper rectangles, squares, triangles, and circle shapes, glue, and paper in the art area. Invite children to create vehicles by gluing the shapes to the papers.

Invite children to create designs using toy vehicles. Have children dip the wheels of toy vehicles in a shallow pan of paint. Then suggest that they "drive" the vehicles around on papers to create designs. Provide pans of several colors for children to use. Display the designs in the art area.

Reading/Writing

Read *Wheel Away!* Have children retell the story in their own words. Encourage them to use position words in their retellings. Then invite children to write a class story about another form of transportation. They might write about a sailboat, a hot-air balloon, or a rocket ship. Suggest they use position words to tell where the vehicle travels. Have children illustrate the story. Post the story and illustrations in the language area.

Arrange for children to ride on a city bus or a school bus. When they return to the classroom, invite children to draw pictures and dictate or write stories about the experience.

Social Studies

Ask children to make a list of traffic rules. Write their responses on chart paper. Some of the responses might include using seat belts, stopping at red lights and stop signs, and looking both ways before crossing streets.

Related Literature

School Bus by Donald Crews. Follow the progress of school buses as they take children to school and bring them home again. Greenwillow, 1984.

Trucks by Gail Gibbons. A variety of trucks that work around us every day is pictured. HarperCollins, 1981.

Wheel Away! by Dayle Ann Dodds. A circular tale of a bicycle wheel that comes loose, rolls down a hill, through a mill, into a lake, over a cake, and all through the town until it rolls up another hill and back to where it came loose. HarperCollins, 1989.

The Wheels on the Bus by Maryann Kovalski. A picture book adaptation of the well-loved song. Little, 1987.

Wheels on the Bus by Raffi. As the rickety old bus collects an odd assortment of passengers in a quaint little town, the reader may join in with the sounds of the bus and motions of the driver and passengers. McKay, 1990.

Where Is Thumbkin?

Where is Thumbkin? Where is Thumbkin? Here I am. Here I am. How are you today, sir? Very well, I thank you. Run away. Run away.

Music Expansion

Invite children to place their hands behind their backs. Have them extend one hand with the thumb up each time they sing "Here I am." When they sing "Run away," have them return that hand behind their backs. Continue singing about pointer, tallman, ringman, pinky, and the family showing the appropriate fingers.

Invite children to sit in a circle. Sing the song substituting one of the children's names for *Thumbkin*. Encourage that child to sing the appropriate lines in response. Also have the child suggest a movement for the entire class to do for the last line. Some movements might include *turn around, shake your head*, or *please stand up*.

Use the song as a greeting to begin the day. Change the words to use children's names. Encourage them to sing their response. The greeting song might be like the one below.

> Where is Linda? *(Teacher sings.)*
> Where is Linda? *(Teacher sings.)*
> Here I am. Here I am. *(Child responds by singing and waving.)*
> How are you today? *(Teacher sings.)*
> Very well, I thank you. *(Child responds.)*
> Clap your hands, clap your hands. *(Entire class sings and claps.)*

Play a hide-and-seek game. Hide an object somewhere in the room. Suggest that children sing as they search for the object. When a child has found the object, invite that child to hide another object. Continue the activity until all interested children have had a chance to hide something.

> Where is the tiger?
> Where is the tiger?
> Where is it? Where is it?
> Let's see who can find it.
> Let's see who can find it.
> Look around. Look around.

Themes

Body
Counting/Numbers
Family
Five Senses
Friends

Featured Book

Hand Rhymes by Marc Brown

Curriculum Integration

Choose activities from the following curriculum areas that fit your teaching style and the needs and interests of the children.

Science

Have magnifying glasses available on the science table so that children can examine their own and their friends' fingers and fingerprints.

Use this song when introducing a unit on the five senses. Provide objects that have different textures or temperatures for children to touch. Encourage children to handle the items. Then place one of the items in a paper bag. Have children reach into the bag, touch the object, and try to identify the item by using only the sense of touch.

Math

Help children count how many thumbs are in class. Children might choose to count by ones or twos.

Invite children to make number books. Have each child assemble five sheets of paper to make a book. Next help children write the numbers 1 through 5 at the top of the pages. Then encourage children to use ink pads and make the appropriate number of thumbprints on each page. Suggest they use markers or crayons to turn the thumbprints into pictures or designs.

Read *Hand Rhymes*. Teach children several of the counting rhymes and the hand actions that accompany each rhyme.

Art

Invite children to use fingerpaints to make pictures or designs. Encourage them to use all of their fingers, thumbs, and the sides of their hands.

Provide different textures of clay. Invite children to work the material with their fingers and hands as they create sculptures.

Reading/Writing

Invite children to write a class story called "The Adventures of Thumbkin." Have them imagine that Thumbkin is a little person no bigger than your thumb. What are Thumbkin's parents like? Where do they live? What adventures does Thumbkin have? When the story is completed, suggest children illustrate their story. Display the story and illustrations on a wall or bulletin board.

Read *Hand Rhymes* to children. Then invite children to make rhymes and hand movements of their own.

Social Studies

Invite children to compare the skin color of their hands with each other. Provide skin-tone paints or crayons. Suggest children trace their hands and then create pictures of hands.

Ask children to brainstorm a list of things that people use their hands to do. Post the list on a wall or bulletin board. Encourage children to talk to their parents and find out how they use their hands in their work. Have children add anything new to the list.

Invite children to pantomime some of the things they do with their hands such as combing hair, brushing teeth, or waving good-bye.

Related Literature

Hand Rhymes by Marc Brown. This collection of nursery rhymes is accompanied by diagrams of finger plays. Penguin, 1985.

My Five Senses by Aliki. This book teaches a child through words and interesting pictures about his or her five senses. HarperCollins, 1989.

My Hands by Aliki. The book describes the parts of the hand and all the things our hands help us to do. HarperCollins, 1990.

Dear Family,

Singing and reading can be two of the most rewarding experiences you share with your child. A child whose day includes rhythmic sounds and lively stories is more apt to grow up loving books. And a child who loves books will want to learn to read them.

The minibook on the attached sheet offers a way to provide the rhythmic sounds and lively stories. It contains the first verse of a well-known children's song, a related activity, and the title of a quality children's picture book. To create the minibook, have your child fold along the dotted line. Next help your child cut the excess paper off the bottom so the edges are even. Then have your child evenly fold the left side over to the right and crease the fold. Your child will enjoy decorating the cover.

The song in the minibook is one that is being used to introduce and reinforce the current classroom theme. Encourage your child to "teach" you the song and any actions associated with it. Sing this song frequently with your child as you go about your daily routines.

Talk about the related activity with your child, and then provide the materials necessary to complete the activity. When your child is finished, talk about what your child did. For example, if he or she drew a picture, ask your child to tell you about it. You might want to write some of your child's comments beside the picture.

The suggested picture book can be found in most public and school libraries and bookstores. Set aside a special time every day to read aloud to your child. Choose a comfortable spot and make sure he or she can see the book clearly. Read slowly with lots of expression and enthusiasm. Make the book come alive, and don't be afraid to ham it up!

Most of all, have fun! There is never a wasted minute when you spend time with your child. The benefits and rewards will have a lasting effect on you both.

Sincerely,

© 1994 Perfection Learning Corporation

A B C D E F G,
H I J K L M N O P,
Q R S,
T U V,
W, X,
Y, and Z.
Now I know my ABCs.
Tell me what you think of me.

Draw a picture of yourself. Then write your name or the letters you hear in your name.

Read *A my name is ALICE* by Jane Bayer.

A-B-C Song

A-hunting we will go.
A-hunting we will go.
We'll catch a fox and put him in a box,
And then we'll let him go.

Draw a picture of something you would put in a box.

Read *The Trek* by Ann Jonas.

A-Hunting We Will Go

© 1994 Perfection Learning Corporation

I'm bringing home a baby bumblebee.
Won't my mommy be so proud of me?
I'm bringing home a baby bumblebee.
Buzzy, wuzzy, wuzzy, wuzzy.
Ouch! He stung me!

Where would you keep a baby bumblebee? Draw a picture of the baby bumblebee in your home.

Read *Over in the Meadow* illustrated by Ezra Jack Keats.

Baby Bumblebee

© 1994 Perfection Learning Corporation

Oh, the bear went over the mountain,
The bear went over the mountain,
The bear went over the mountain
To see what he could see.
And all that he could see,
And all that he could see
Was the other side of the mountain,
The other side of the mountain,
The other side of the mountain
Was all that he could see.

Draw a picture of what you think the bear might have seen on the other side of the mountain.

Read *Corduroy* by Don Freeman.

The Bear Went Over the Mountain

© 1994 Perfection Learning Corporation

There was a farmer had a dog,
And Bingo was his name-o.
B-I-N-G-O,
B-I-N-G-O,
B-I-N-G-O,
And Bingo was his name-o.

What do you think Bingo looks like? Draw a picture of him.

Read *Pet Show!* by Ezra Jack Keats.

Bingo

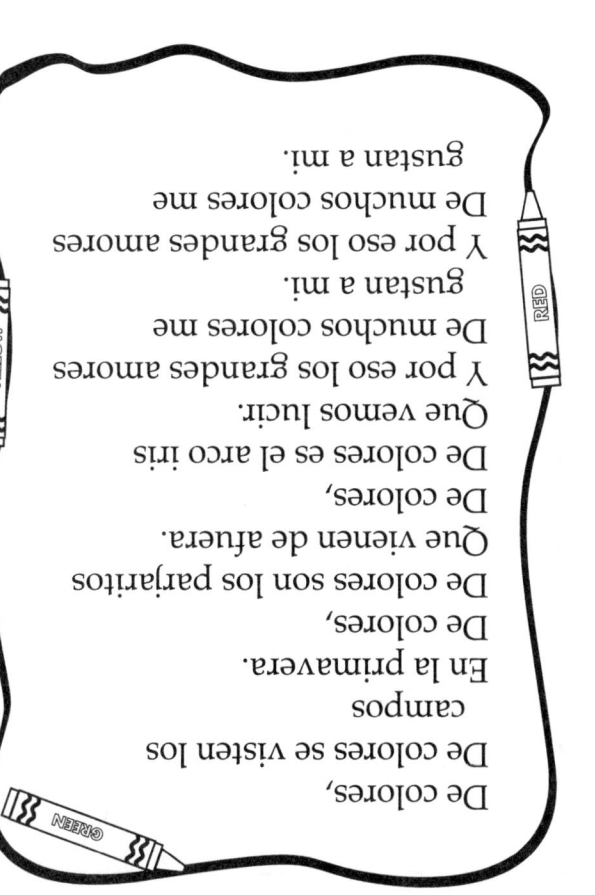

De colores,
De colores se visten los campos
En la primavera.
De colores,
De colores son los pajaritos
Que vienen de afuera.
De colores,
De colores es el arco iris
Que vemos lucir.
Y por eso los grandes amores
De muchos colores me
gustan a mí.
Y por eso los grandes amores
De muchos colores me
gustan a mí.

What is your favorite color? Draw a picture of something that color.

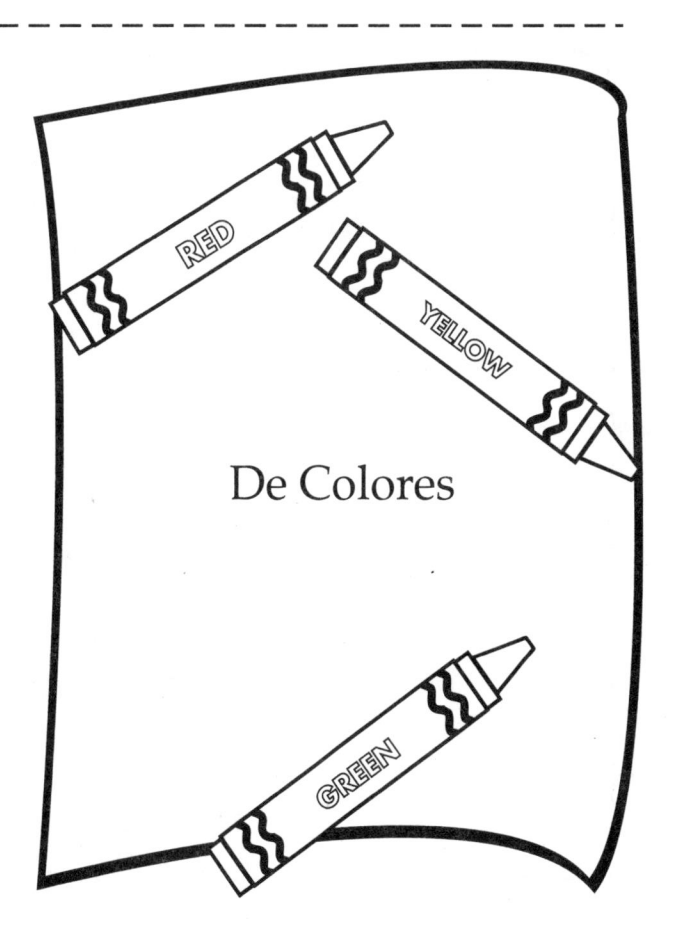

Read *is it red? is it yellow? is it blue?* by Tana Hoban.

De Colores

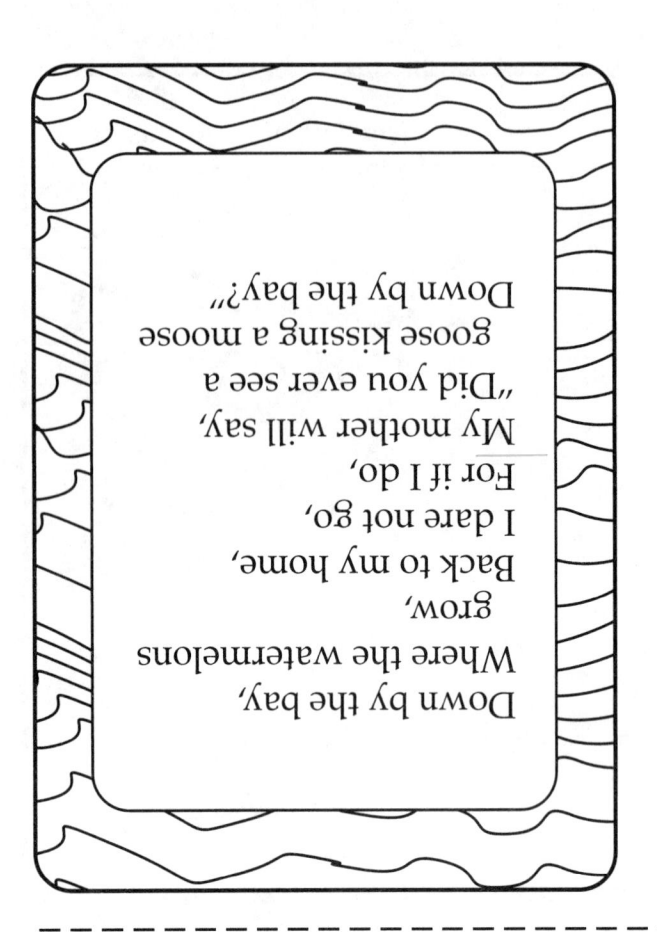

Draw what you might see down by the bay.

Down by the bay,
Where the watermelons grow,
Back to my home,
I dare not go,
For if I do,
My mother will say,
"Did you ever see a goose kissing a moose
Down by the bay?"

Read *17 Kings and 42 Elephants* by Margaret Mahy.

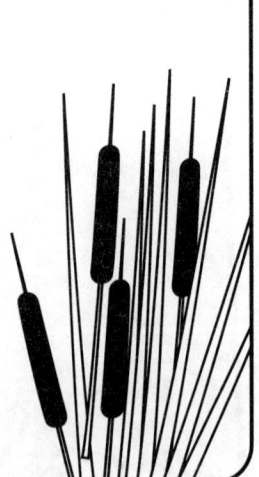

Down by the Bay

© 1994 Perfection Learning Corporation

176

The eency, weency spider
went up the water spout.
Down came the rain and
washed the spider out.
Out came the sun and
dried up all the rain,
And the eency, weency
spider went up the spout
again.

What do you think an eency, weency spider looks like? Draw a picture of it.

Read *Anansi the Spider: a tale from the Ashanti* by Gerald McDermott.

The Eency Weency Spider

© 1994 Perfection Learning Corporation 177

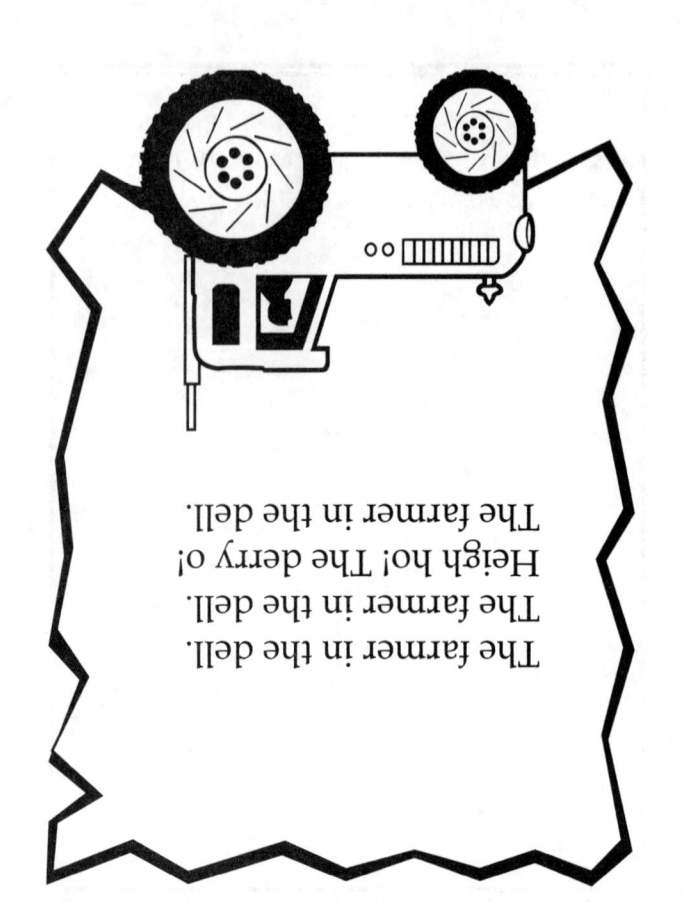

The farmer in the dell.
The farmer in the dell.
Heigh ho! The derry o!
The farmer in the dell.

Draw something you might find on a farm.

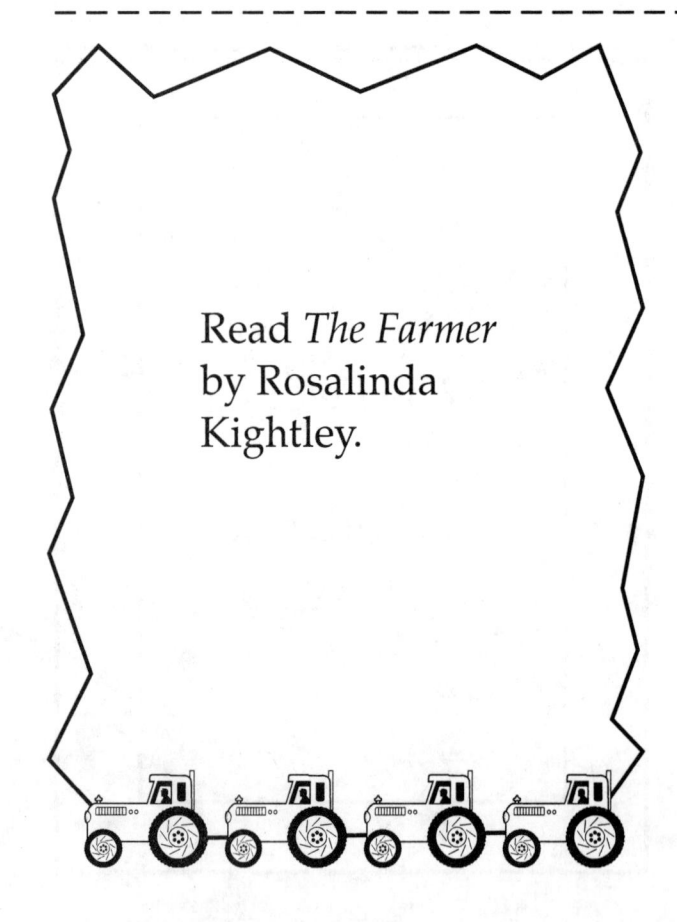

Read *The Farmer* by Rosalinda Kightley.

The Farmer in the Dell

He's got the whole world
in His hands.
He's got the whole world
in His hands.
He's got the whole world
in His hands.
He's got the whole world
in His hands.

Tell about something you can do to help keep the world beautiful using pictures or words.

Read *People* by Peter Spier.

He's Got the Whole World

© 1994 Perfection Learning Corporation

Head and shoulders,
knees and toes,
Knees and toes.
Head and shoulders,
knees and toes,
Knees and toes.
Eyes and ears and
mouth and nose,
Head and shoulders,
knees and toes,
Knees and toes.

Cut out pictures of parts of the body from magazines and glue them in the space above to make a collage.

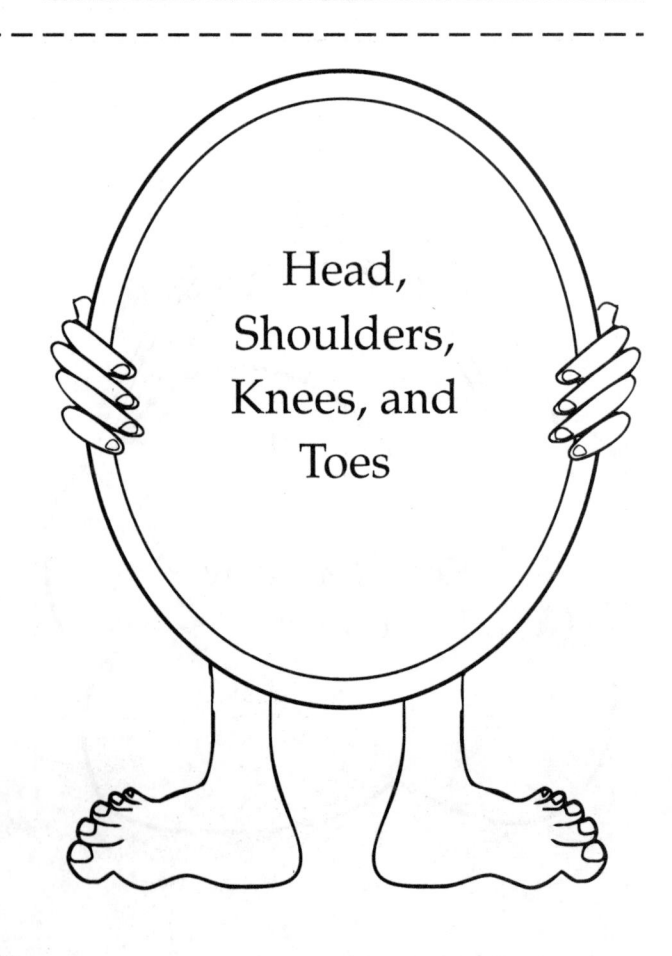

Read *Here Are My Hands* by Bill Martin Jr. and John Archambault.

Head, Shoulders, Knees, and Toes

© 1994 Perfection Learning Corporation

180

Hickety, tickety bumblebee.
Can you sing your name to me?

What do you think a Hickety, Tickety Bumblebee looks like? Draw a picture of one.

Read *The Icky Bug Counting Book* by Jerry Pallotta.

Hickety Tickety Bumblebee

© 1994 Perfection Learning Corporation

Hickory dickory dock.
The mouse ran up the clock.
The clock struck one,
The mouse ran down.
Hickory dickory dock.

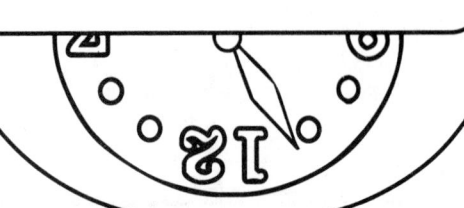

Draw a picture of where you think the mouse went after it ran down the clock.

Read *Nicola Bayley's Book of Nursery Rhymes* by Nicola Bayley.

Hickory Dickory Dock

If you're happy and you
know it,
Clap your hands.
If you're happy and you
know it,
Clap your hands.
Then your face will surely
show it,
If you're happy and you
know it,
Clap your hands.

Draw something that makes you happy.

Read *the temper tantrum book* by Edna Mitchell Preston.

If You're Happy and You Know It

Jack and Jill went up the hill
To fetch a pail of water.
Jack fell down
And broke his crown,
And Jill came tumbling after.

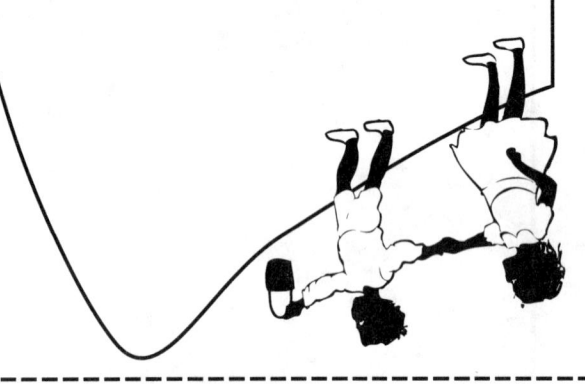

Draw a picture of a pail that Jack and Jill might have used. Decorate it.

Read *Tikki Tikki Tembo* retold by Arlene Mosel.

Jack and Jill

© 1994 Perfection Learning Corporation

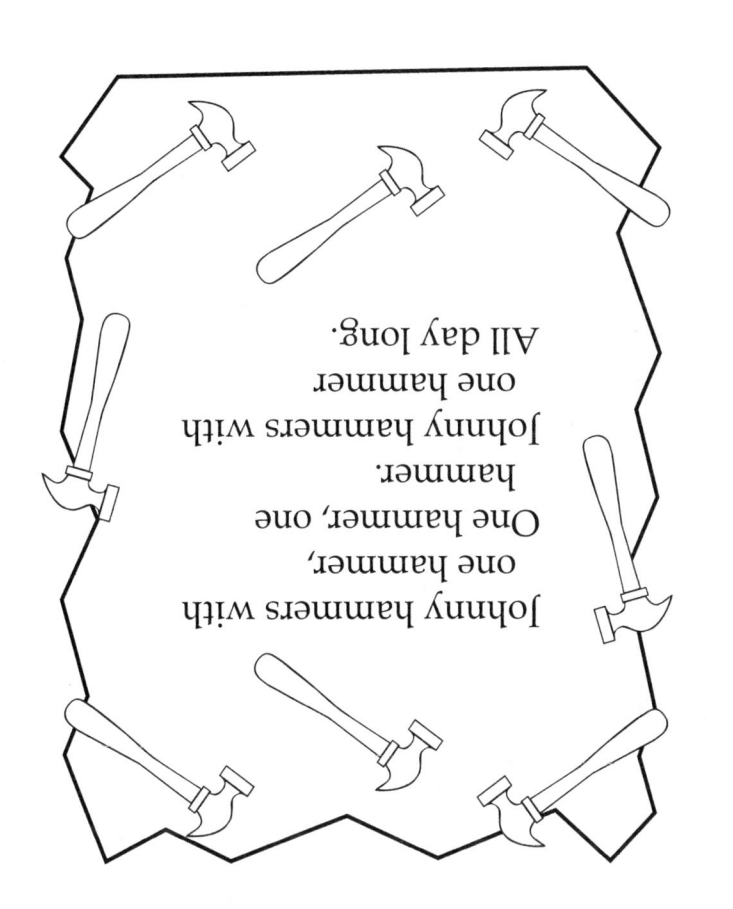

Johnny hammers with one hammer,
One hammer, one hammer.
Johnny hammers with one hammer
All day long.

What do you think Johnny was hammering? Draw a picture of it.

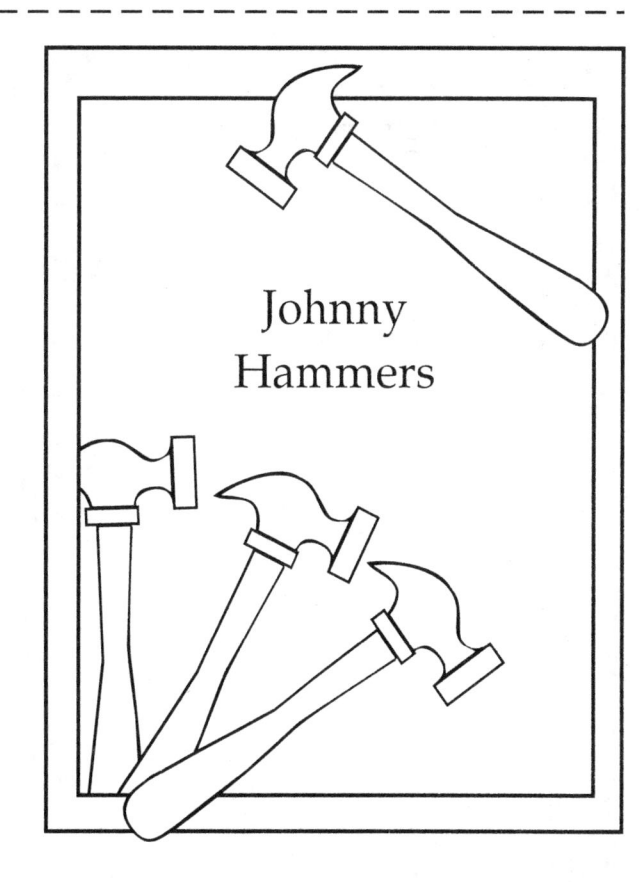

Read *Building a House* by Byron Barton.

Johnny Hammers

© 1994 Perfection Learning Corporation   185

Kumbaya my Lord,
Kumbaya.
Kumbaya my Lord,
Kumbaya.
Kumbaya my Lord,
Kumbaya.
Oh, Lord, Kumbaya.

Kumbaya means *come by here*. Draw a friend coming by your house to play.

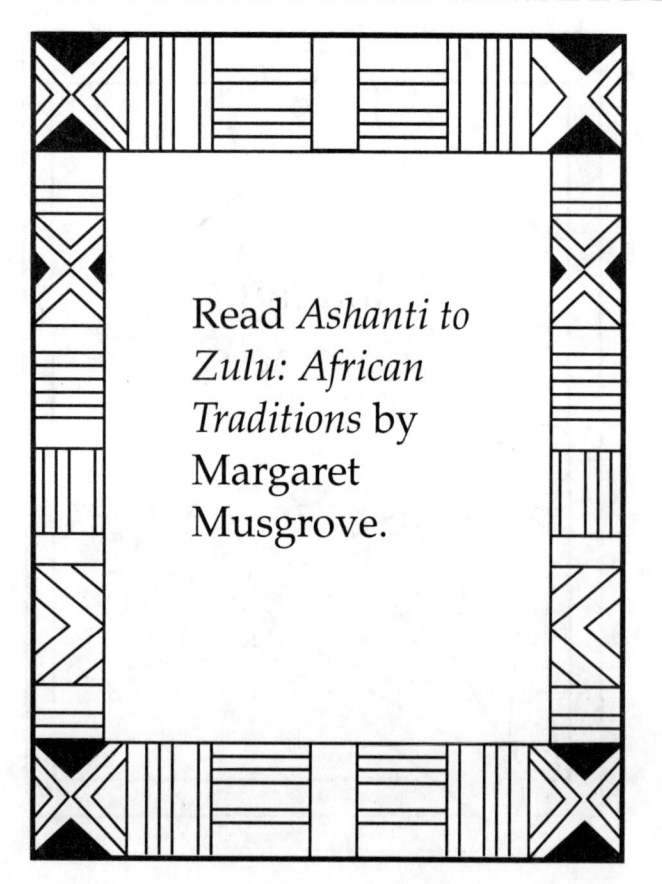

Read *Ashanti to Zulu: African Traditions* by Margaret Musgrove.

Kumbaya

© 1994 Perfection Learning Corporation 186

Little Bunny Foo Foo,
Hopping through the forest,
Scooping up the field mice
And bopping 'em on the head.
Down came the good fairy, and she said:
Little Bunny Foo Foo,
I don't want to see you
Scooping up the field mice
And bopping 'em on the head.
I'll give you three chances, and if you don't behave, I'll turn you into a goon!

The good fairy turned Little Bunny Foo Foo into a goon. Draw a picture of the good fairy or the goon.

Read *Foolish Rabbit's Big Mistake* by Rafe Martin.

Little Bunny Foo Foo

© 1994 Perfection Learning Corporation 187

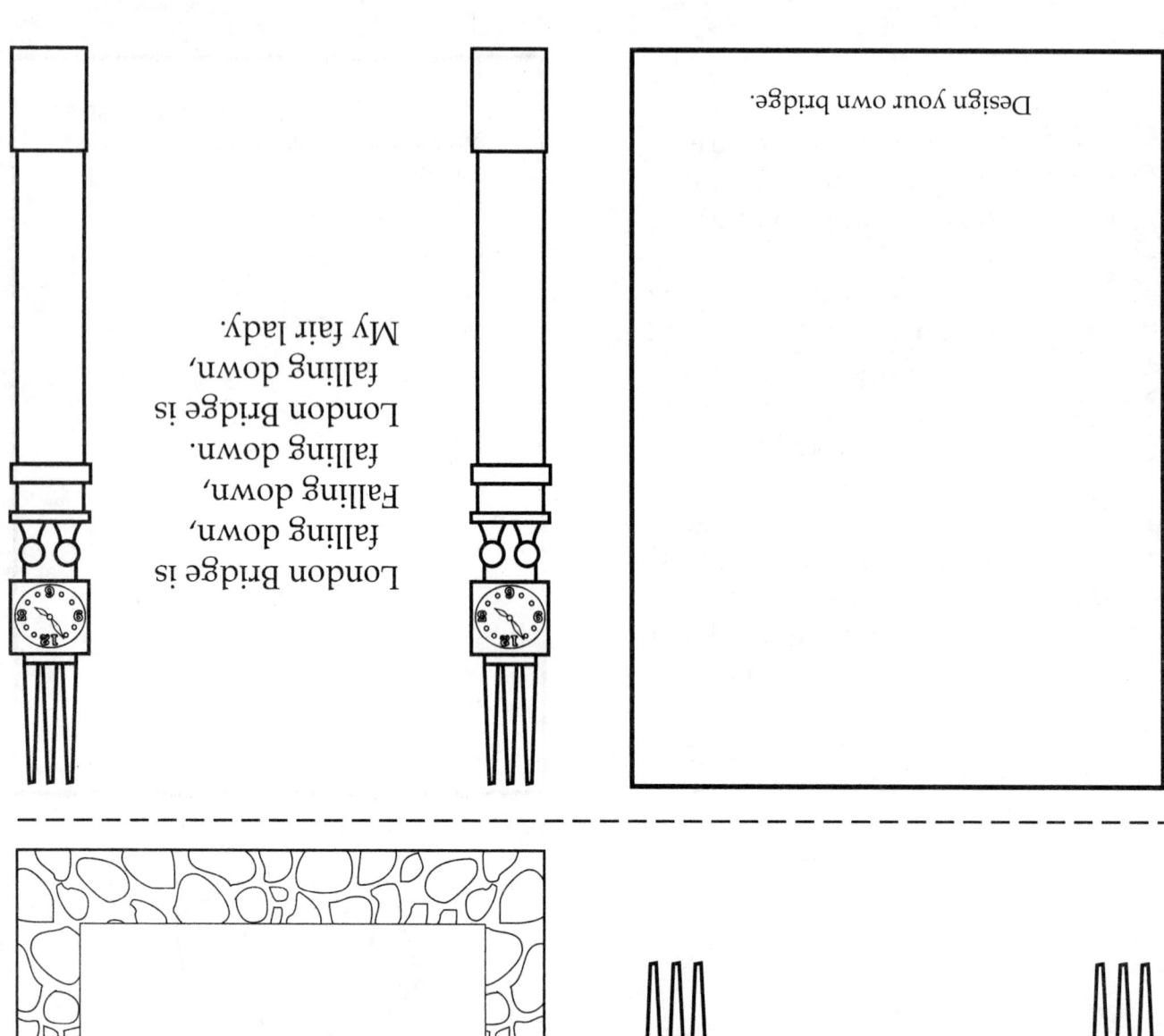

London Bridge is falling down,
Falling down,
falling down.
London Bridge is falling down,
My fair lady.

Design your own bridge.

Read *The Three Billy Goats Gruff* retold by Paul Galdone.

London Bridge

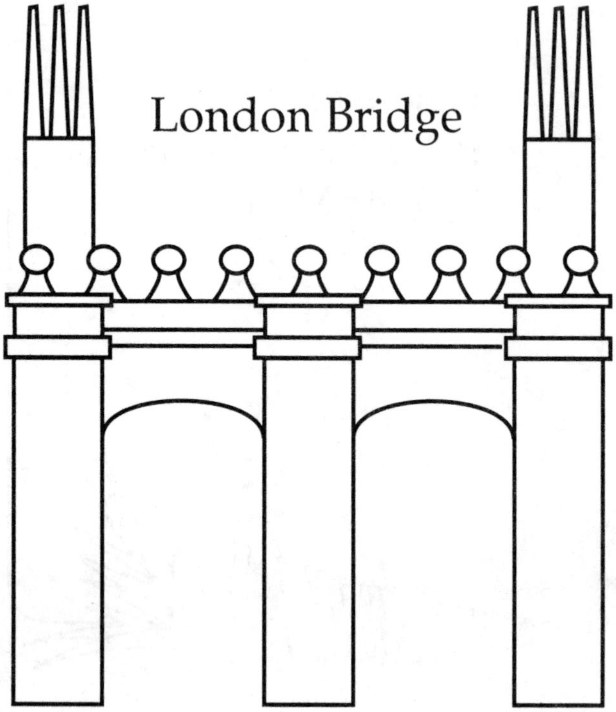

© 1994 Perfection Learning Corporation   **188**

Mary's wearing a red dress,
A red dress, a red dress.
Mary's wearing a red dress
All day long.

Draw a picture of yourself wearing something special.

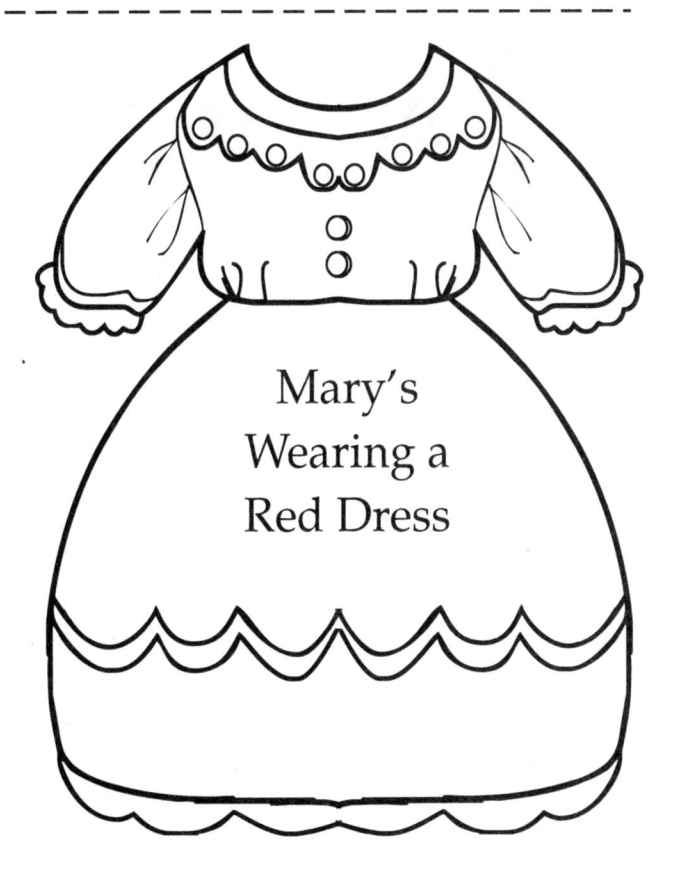

Read *Quick as a Cricket* by Audrey Wood.

Mary's Wearing a Red Dress

© 1994 Perfection Learning Corporation

Miss Polly had a dolly who was sick, sick, sick.
So she called for the doctor to come quick, quick, quick.
The doctor came with his bag and his hat.
And he knocked on the door with a rat-tat-tat.

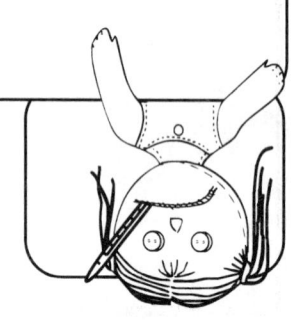

Draw a picture of Miss Polly's sick dolly.

Read *The Berenstain Bears Go to the Doctor* by Stan and Jan Berenstain.

Miss Polly Had a Dolly

© 1994 Perfection Learning Corporation

190

The more we are together,
together, together,
The more we are together
the happier we'll be.
For your friends are my
friends, and my friends
are your friends.
The more we are together
the happier we'll be.

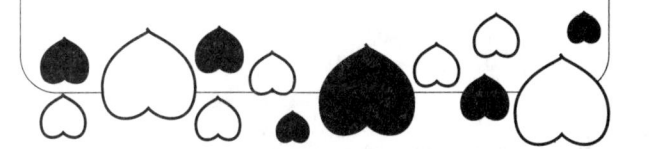

Draw a picture of you and a friend playing together.

Read *May I Bring a Friend?* by Beatrice Schenk de Regniers.

The More We Are Together

© 1994 Perfection Learning Corporation **191**

Oh, do you know the
muffin man,
The muffin man, the
muffin man?
Oh, do you know the
muffin man
Who lives on Drury
Lane?

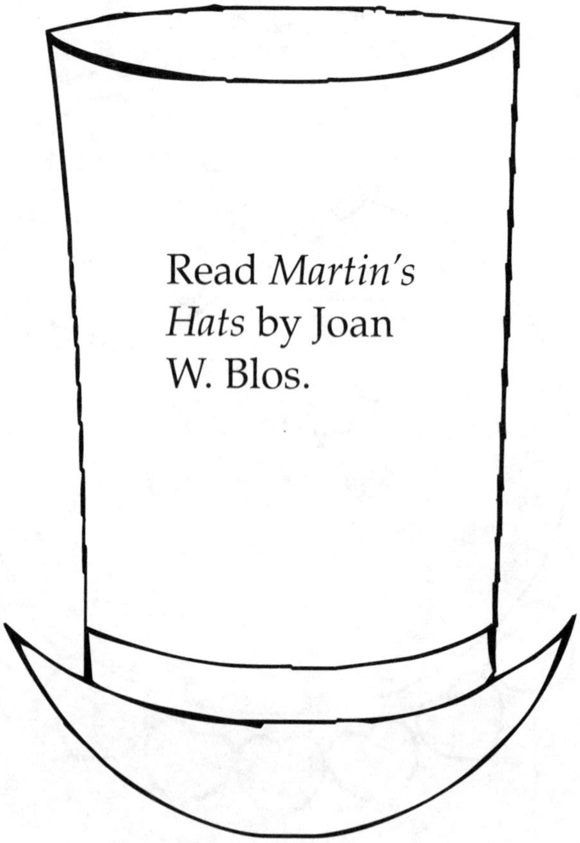

What do you think the muffin man looks like? Draw a picture of him.

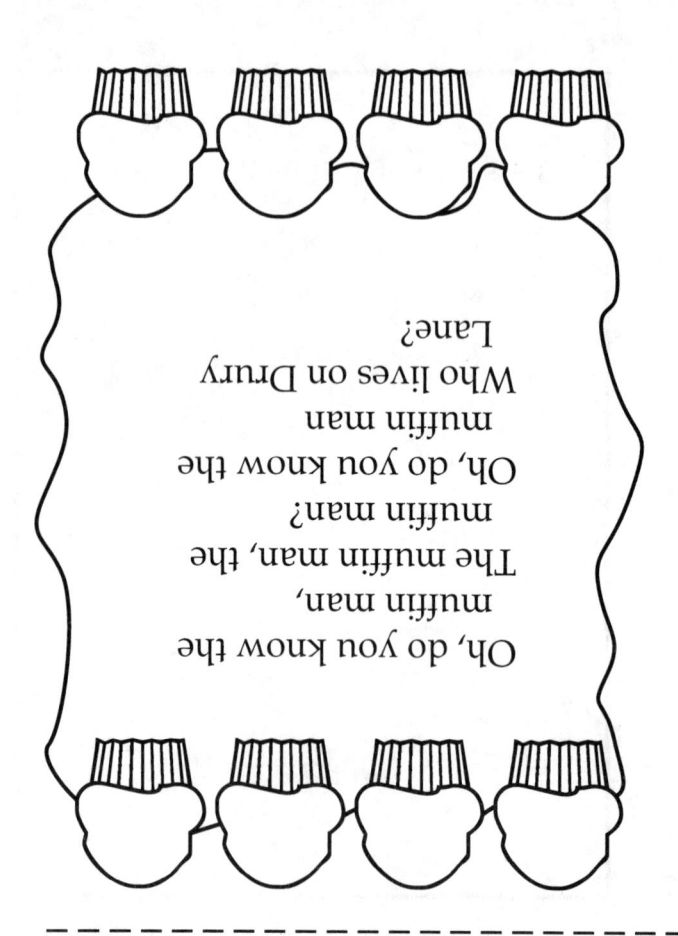

Read *Martin's Hats* by Joan W. Blos.

The Muffin Man

© 1994 Perfection Learning Corporation

Old MacDonald had a farm,
E-I-E-I-O.
And on his farm he had some chicks,
E-I-E-I-O.
With a chick, chick here
And a chick, chick there.
Here a chick, there a chick,
Everywhere a chick, chick.
Old MacDonald had a farm,
E-I-E-I-O.

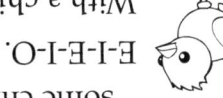

Old MacDonald had many things on his farm. Draw a picture of something on his farm.

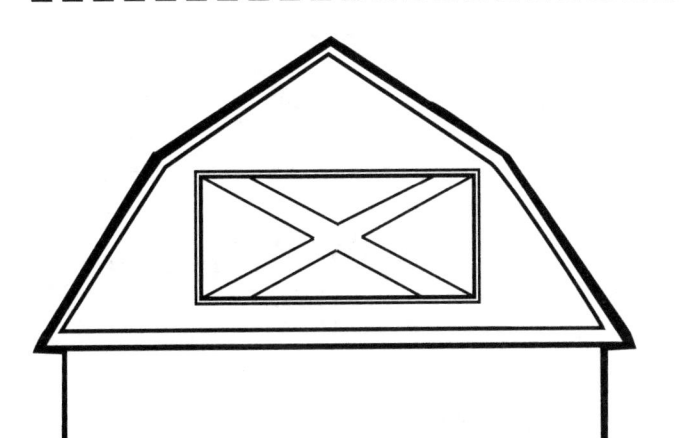

Read *Barn Dance!* by Bill Martin Jr. and John Archambault.

Old MacDonald

© 1994 Perfection Learning Corporation

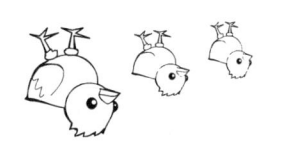

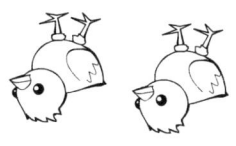

193

Where, oh where is
dear little Johnny?
Where, oh where is
dear little Johnny?
Where, oh where is
dear little Johnny?
Way down yonder in
the pawpaw patch.

What do you think a pawpaw looks like? Draw a picture of it.

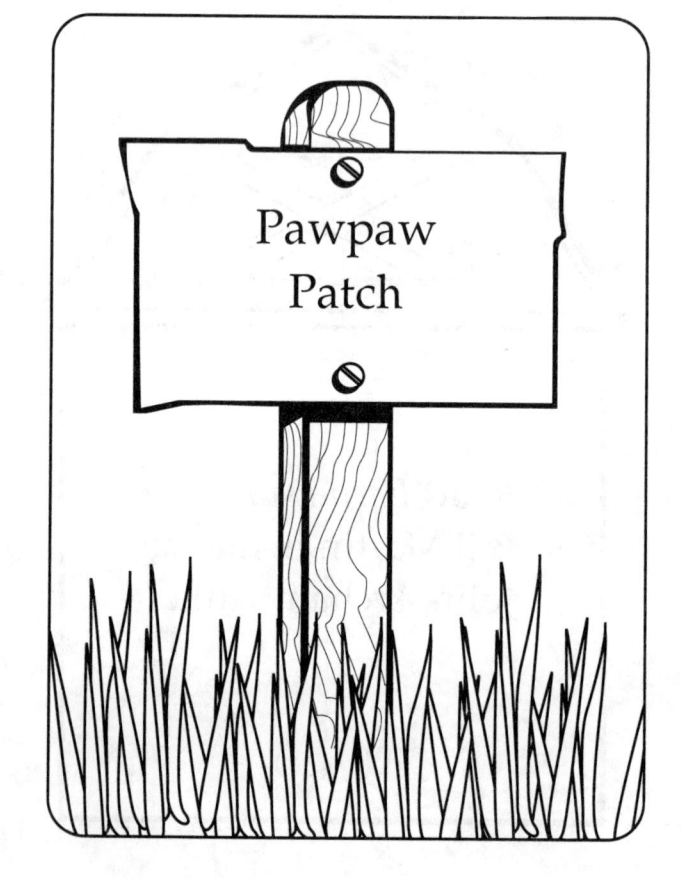

Read *Growing Vegetable Soup* by Lois Ehlert.

Pawpaw Patch

© 1994 Perfection Learning Corporation

All around the cobbler's bench
The monkey chased the weasel.
The monkey thought 'twas all in fun.
Pop! goes the weasel.

Design a pair of shoes that you would like to wear.

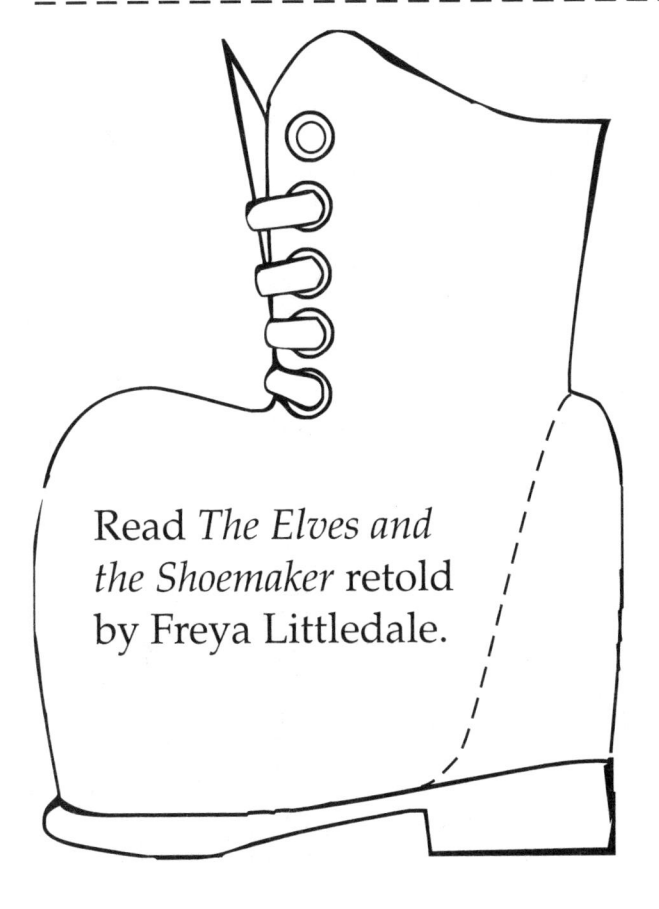

Read *The Elves and the Shoemaker* retold by Freya Littledale.

Pop Goes the Weasel

© 1994 Perfection Learning Corporation

Ring around the rosy,
Pocket full of posies.
Ashes, ashes,
We all fall down!

Posies is another name for flowers.
Draw a picture of some flowers.

Read *Rosie's Walk* by Pat Hutchins.

Ring Around the Rosy

© 1994 Perfection Learning Corporation   196

Row, row, row your boat
Gently down the stream.
Merrily, merrily, merrily, merrily,
Life is but a dream.

If you had a boat, what would it look like? Draw a picture of it.

Read *Harbor* by Donald Crews.

Row, Row, Row Your Boat

© 1994 Perfection Learning Corporation

Shalom means *hello, good-bye,* or *peace.*
Draw a picture of yourself saying
"shalom" to someone.

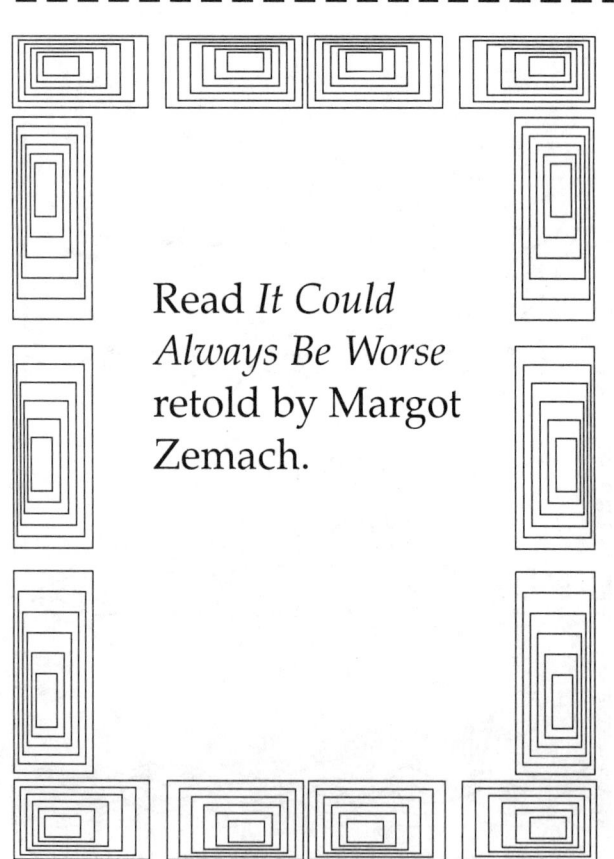

Shalom, chavarim,
Shalom, chavarim,
Shalom, shalom.
L'hitra-ot, L'hitra-ot,
Shalom, shalom.

Read *It Could Always Be Worse* retold by Margot Zemach.

Shalom Chavarim

© 1994 Perfection Learning Corporation

She'll be coming 'round the mountain when she comes.
She'll be coming 'round the mountain,
She'll be coming 'round the mountain,
She'll be coming 'round the mountain when she comes.
She'll be coming 'round the mountain when she comes.

Who is she? Draw a picture of the person who comes around the mountain.

Read *Things That Go* by Anne Rockwell.

She'll Be Coming 'Round the Mountain

© 1994 Perfection Learning Corporation 199

There was an old lady
who swallowed a fly.
I don't why she swallowed
a fly.
Perhaps she'll die.
There was an old lady who
swallowed a spider
That wriggled and jiggled
and tickled inside her.
She swallowed the spider to
catch the fly.
I don't know why she
swallowed the fly.
Perhaps she'll die.

The old lady swallowed unusual things. Draw a picture of something that would be good for her to swallow.

Read *I Know a Lady* by Charlotte Zolotow.

There Was an Old Lady

© 1994 Perfection Learning Corporation

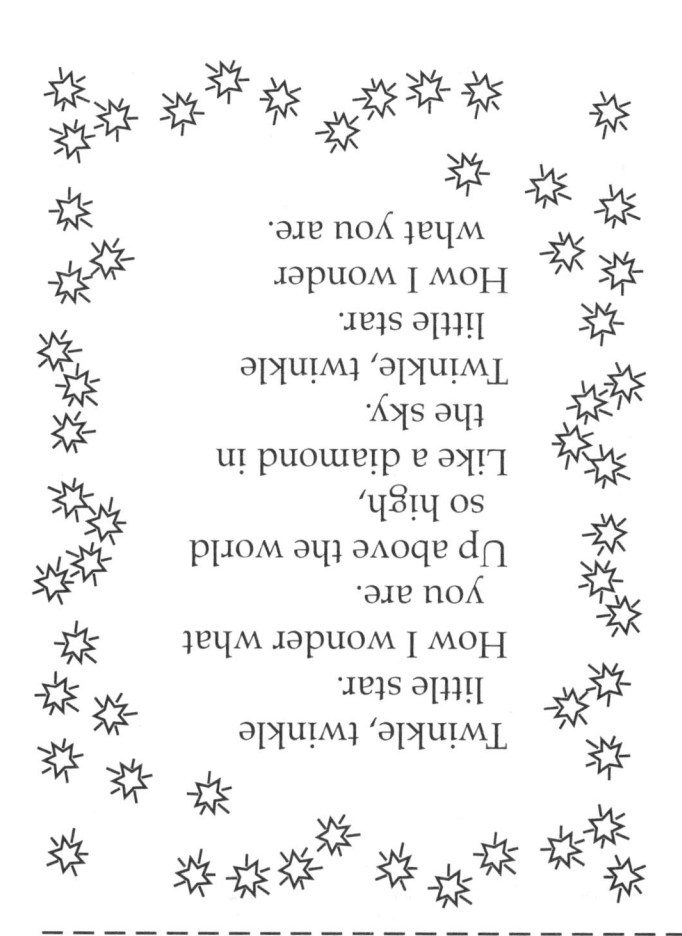

Twinkle, twinkle
little star.
How I wonder what
you are.
Up above the world
so high,
Like a diamond in
the sky.
Twinkle, twinkle
little star.
How I wonder
what you are.

Draw a picture of something you might see at night.

Read *Grandfather Twilight* by Barbara Berger.

Twinkle, Twinkle Little Star

© 1994 Perfection Learning Corporation 201

Draw a picture of something with wheels.

The wheels on
the bus go
'round and 'round,
'Round and 'round,
'round and 'round.'
The wheels on the
bus go 'round and
'round,
All through
the town.

Read *Wheel Away!* by Dayle Ann Dodds.

The Wheels on the Bus

© 1994 Perfection Learning Corporation   202

Where is Thumbkin?
Where is Thumbkin?
Here I am. Here I am.
How are you today, sir?
Very well, I thank you.
Run away. Run away.

Press your thumb onto a stamp pad and then on paper. Decorate your thumbprint to create an animal, person, flower, or anything you like.

Read *Hand Rhymes* by Marc Brown.

Where Is Thumbkin?

© 1994 Perfection Learning Corporation

Glossary

Art Media — Any type of materials used for creating art projects. These can include paint, chalk, crayon, torn paper, collage materials, and so on.

Brainstorm — A cooperative effort by the children to list everything they know about a subject. As children brainstorm, write their ideas on chart paper or the chalkboard.

Collage — A term for an art project in which a variety of materials or objects are glued in creative ways onto another surface.

Collage Materials — A variety of materials used on collages such as fabric and paper scraps, ribbon, pom-poms, yarn, sequins, glitter, and so on.

Dictate — The process of having young children tell an adult what they want written down. The adult writes the children's words exactly as they are spoken.

Graph — A mathematical means of collecting information for purposes such as making comparisons or reinforcing the concepts of *most, more, less, fewer, longest, longer,* and *shortest*. A graph can be made by taping a square grid on a tarp or the floor or by drawing a grid on a large piece of paper.

Interest Centers — Areas set up around the room for activities such as housekeeping, block building, manipulatives, science, writing, and art. Provide children with a time when they may explore these interest centers.

Invented Spelling — A means of spelling using letters that represent the sounds children hear instead of actual correct spellings.

continued

Pitch — The high or low tone of a voice.

Rhyme Bank — A list of rhyming words to facilitate writing songs or poems. Place the words on chart paper and display them in a visible part of the room.

Rhythm Instruments — The instruments referred to in this book are percussion instruments. They might include rhythm sticks, wood blocks, jingle bells, maracas, and castanets.

Seriate — To put items in order according to a system of classification, often by size or weight.

Tempo — The rate of speed of the music or activity.

Theme Index

The theme index makes it possible for teachers to select a theme and find the Music Explosion song that can be used to introduce or support that particular theme.

Alphabet
A-B-C Song
Twinkle, Twinkle Little Star

Animals
A-Hunting We Will Go
Baby Bumblebee
Bingo
Down by the Bay
The Farmer in the Dell
Hickory Dickory Dock
Kumbaya
Little Bunny Foo Foo
Old MacDonald
Pop Goes the Weasel
There Was an Old Lady

Bears
The Bear Went Over the Mountain

Bodies of Water
Down by the Bay
Row, Row, Row Your Boat

Body
Head, Shoulders, Knees, and Toes
Where Is Thumbkin?

Clothing
Mary's Wearing a Red Dress
Pop Goes the Weasel

Colors
De Colores
Mary's Wearing a Red Dress

Community Helpers
The Farmer in the Dell
Johnny Hammers
Miss Polly Had a Dolly
The Muffin Man
Pop Goes the Weasel

Construction
Johnny Hammers
London Bridge

Counting/Numbers
De Colores
Down by the Bay
The Eency Weency Spider
Hickety Tickety Bumblebee
Hickory Dickory Dock
Johnny Hammers
Twinkle, Twinkle Little Star
Where Is Thumbkin?

Cultures
De Colores
The Eency Weency Spider
He's Got the Whole World
Kumbaya
Shalom Chavarim

Drug Awareness
Miss Polly Had a Dolly

Ecology
He's Got the Whole World

continued

Emotions/Feelings
If You're Happy and You Know It
Kumbaya
Mary's Wearing a Red Dress

Endangered Species
A-Hunting We Will Go

Family
The Farmer in the Dell
The More We Are Together
She'll Be Coming 'Round the
   Mountain
Where Is Thumbkin?

Farms
The Farmer in the Dell
Old MacDonald

Five Senses
Where Is Thumbkin?

Folklore and Tales
The Eency Weency Spider
London Bridge

Food/Nutrition
The Farmer in the Dell
The Muffin Man
There Was an Old Lady

Friends
He's Got the Whole World
The More We Are Together
Pawpaw Patch
Ring Around the Rosy
Shalom Chavarim
Where Is Thumbkin?

Growing Things
Down by the Bay
The Farmer in the Dell
Hickety Tickety Bumblebee
Old MacDonald
Pawpaw Patch

Habitats
A-Hunting We Will Go
Baby Bumblebee
The Bear Went Over the Mountain
Little Bunny Foo Foo

Health
The Farmer in the Dell
Head, Shoulders, Knees, and Toes
Miss Polly Had a Dolly
The Muffin Man
There Was an Old Lady

Hibernation
The Bear Went Over the Mountain

Holidays
Shalom Chavarim

Insects
The Eency Weency Spider
Hickety Tickety Bumblebee
There Was an Old Lady

Letters, Words, and Books
A-B-C Song

Night
Twinkle, Twinkle Little Star

continued

Nursery Rhymes
Hickory Dickory Dock
Jack and Jill
London Bridge
Twinkle, Twinkle Little Star

Pets/Pet Care
Bingo

Position Words
The Eency Weency Spider
Hickory Dickory Dock
Jack and Jill
London Bridge
Pawpaw Patch
Ring Around the Rosy
The Wheels on the Bus

Rhyming Words
A-Hunting We Will Go
Down by the Bay

Self-Awareness
He's Got the Whole World
Head, Shoulders, Knees, and Toes
If You're Happy and You Know It
Mary's Wearing a Red Dress

Shapes
The More We Are Together
Ring Around the Rosy
Shalom Chavarim
Twinkle, Twinkle Little Star

Simple Machines
Jack and Jill
The Wheels on the Bus

Spiders
The Eency Weency Spider

Time
Hickory Dickory Dock
The More We Are Together

Transportation
Row, Row, Row Your Boat
She'll Be Coming 'Round the Mountain
The Wheels on the Bus